# AMERICAN FOOTBALL

## THE GAME

by Joseph Gladstone

illustrated by Martin Proctor
cover art by Don Kletke
research assistant: George "the Duke" Miller
typesetting by International Typesetting

Merdyne Books • New York

European Distributor: Benson Books, Fakenham, Norfolk

ISBN: 0-934299-18-8

# AMERICAN FOOTBALL

## CONTENTS

# AMERICAN FOOTBALL

# AMERICAN FOOTBALL

## THE GAME

# AMERICAN FOOTBALL

## INTRODUCTION

The *blitz, sacking, the bomb, offense, defence, attack strategies, a rocket, platoons, recruits . . .* an army at war? No, just the everyday terms used in one of the most violent sports played today — American Football!

Vince Lombardi, considered by many experts to be the greatest football coach ever (others point to his mentor, for many years the coach for Army, a university that trains officers, Earl Black) summed up American football as "a symbol of what's best in American life . . . courage, stamina and teamwork." He later amended that to "football is for madmen."

Between November 6, 1869, when that first game of football was played at Rutgers, an American University, and today, the rules and the way the game is played have constantly changed. While, at first, the game appears complex, with this book as your guide, you'll quickly realize American football is an easy sport to follow, understand and enjoy.

The layout of the information in the book follows the game from coin toss to touchdown. There is a trivia question on almost every page and its answer on the following page.

Where strategy plays an important part of a decision, one of our coaches in the "Coaches' Corner" will give you some of the background thinking that goes into the decision.

We know the facts and information provided will increase your understanding and enjoyment of the game. But beware! there are dangers for the true fan . . .

We heard that the wife of one man, who was watching his fifth game of the weekend on TV, stood in front of the set and sobbed, *"You love your football more than me."* He looked up and quietly answered, *"True, but I love you more than baseball!"*

WHAT TEAMS PLAYED IN THAT FIRST GAME AT RUTGERS? WHAT WAS THE FINAL SCORE?

## A QUICK OVERVIEW

### What Are The Teams Trying To Do?

Two teams, each with 11 players on the field at a time, try to score points. The team with the most points at the end of the game is the winner.

### How Do They Score Points?

To score points, a team carries or kicks the football across the opposing team's goal line.

Touchdown . . . . . . . . . . . . . . . . 6 points
Conversion (kick) . . . . . . . . . . . 1 point
                (kicked after a touchdown)
Conversion (pass or run) . . . . . 2 points
                (tried after a touchdown)
Field Goal . . . . . . . . . . . . . . . . . 3 points
Safety . . . . . . . . . . . . . . . . . . . . 2 points

★ ★ ★ ★ TRIVIA ANSWER ★ ★ ★ ★
★     RUTGERS DEFEATED     ★
★        PRINCETON       ★
★          6 TO 4        ★
★ ★ ★ ★ ★ ★ ★ ★ ★ ★ ★ ★ ★ ★ ★ ★

# AMERICAN FOOTBALL

## How Long Is A Game?

An American Pro-Football game is 60 playing minutes long. This hour is divided into 4 fifteen minute quarters with a 15 minute rest period at the half-way mark.

There are many "time-outs" called during a game which stop the official clock, so a game usually takes about 2½ hours to play.

If, at the end of 60 playing minutes, the score is tied, one or more 15 minute, sudden-death overtime quarters are played. *Sudden-death* means the first team to score wins ... the quarter is not finished, the game is over.

# AMERICAN FOOTBALL

## What Do They Use?   The Ball

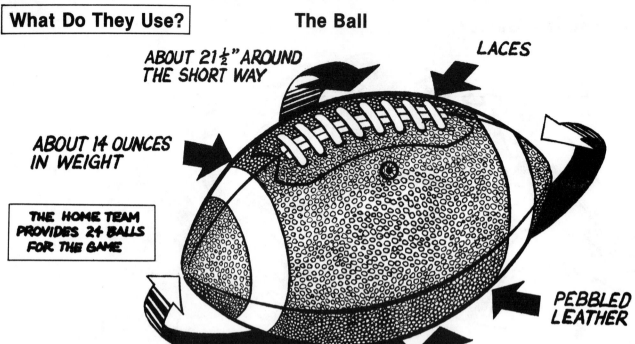

ABOUT 21½" AROUND THE SHORT WAY

LACES

ABOUT 14 OUNCES IN WEIGHT

THE HOME TEAM PROVIDES 24 BALLS FOR THE GAME

PEBBLED LEATHER

ABOUT 28½" AROUND THE LONG WAY

The ball is an oval, pointed at each end, made of a pebble-finished leather.

## The Goal Posts

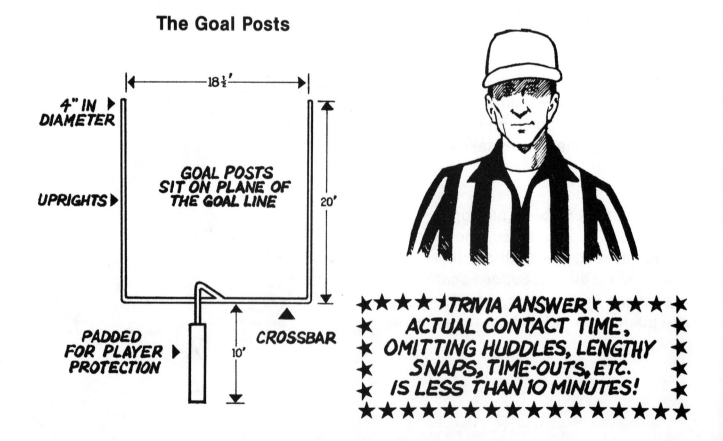

18½'

4" IN DIAMETER

UPRIGHTS ▶

GOAL POSTS SIT ON PLANE OF THE GOAL LINE

20'

PADDED FOR PLAYER PROTECTION ▶

CROSSBAR

10'

★★★★ TRIVIA ANSWER ★★★★
ACTUAL CONTACT TIME, OMITTING HUDDLES, LENGTHY SNAPS, TIME-OUTS, ETC. IS LESS THAN 10 MINUTES!

# AMERICAN FOOTBALL

## Where Do They Play?

The playing field is basically a rectangle, 120 yards by 53-1/3 yards, with goal posts at each end.

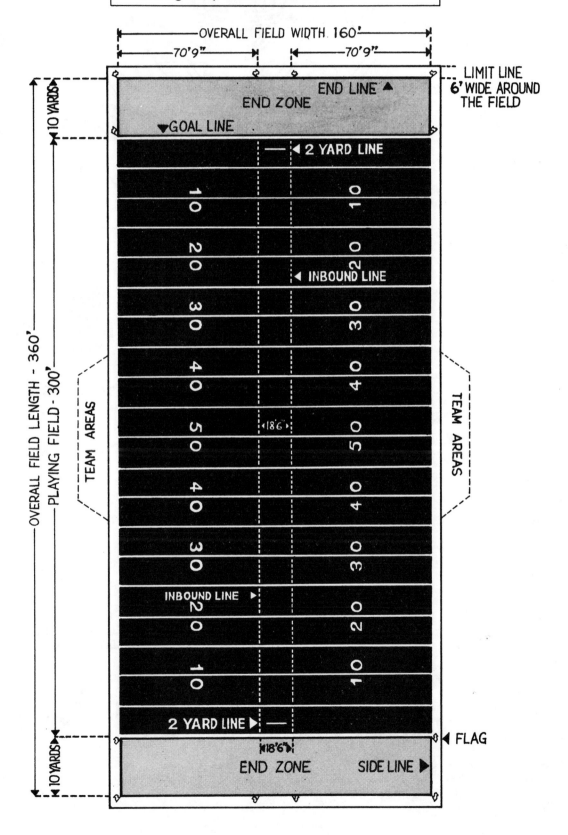

# AMERICAN FOOTBALL

## What Do They Wear?

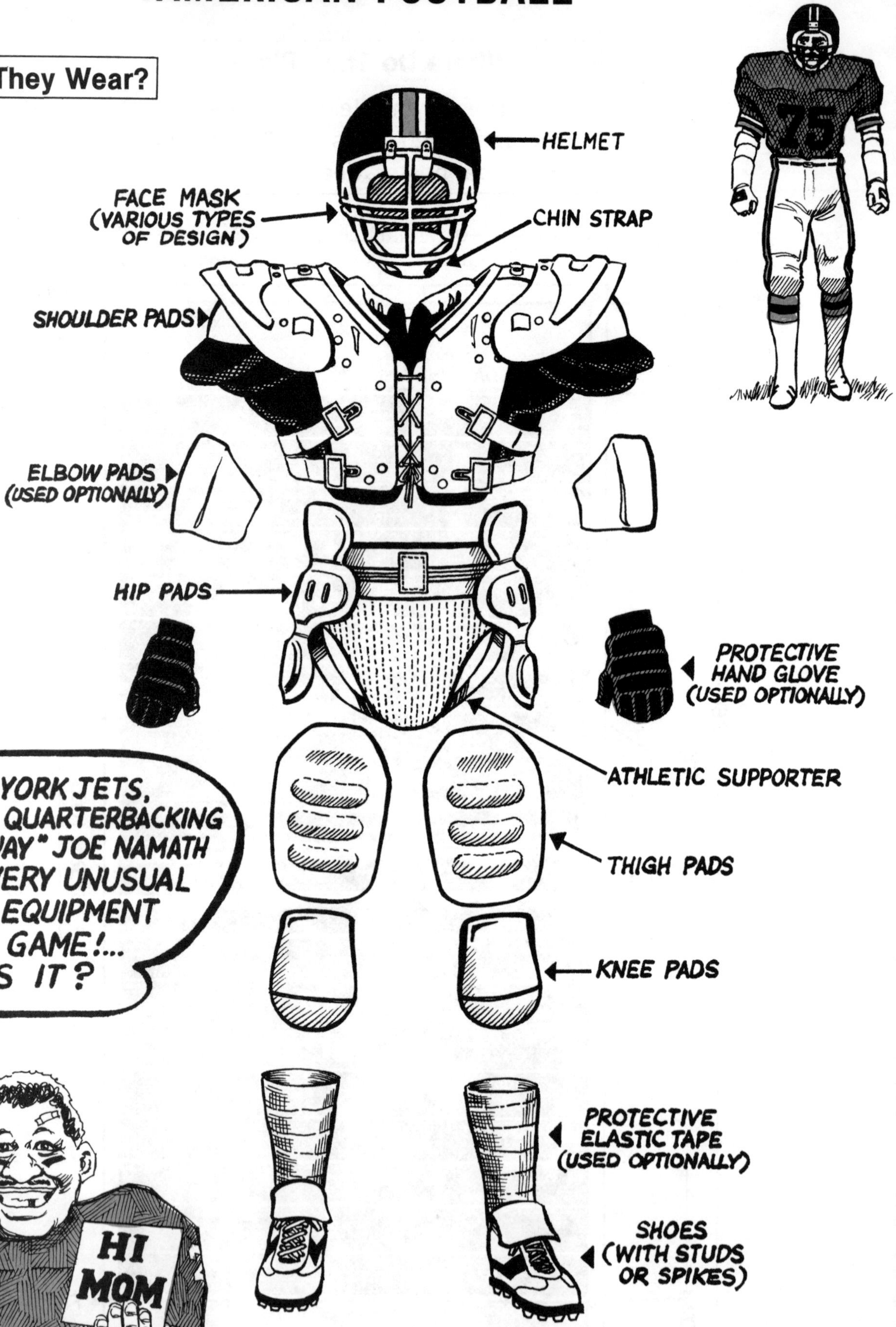


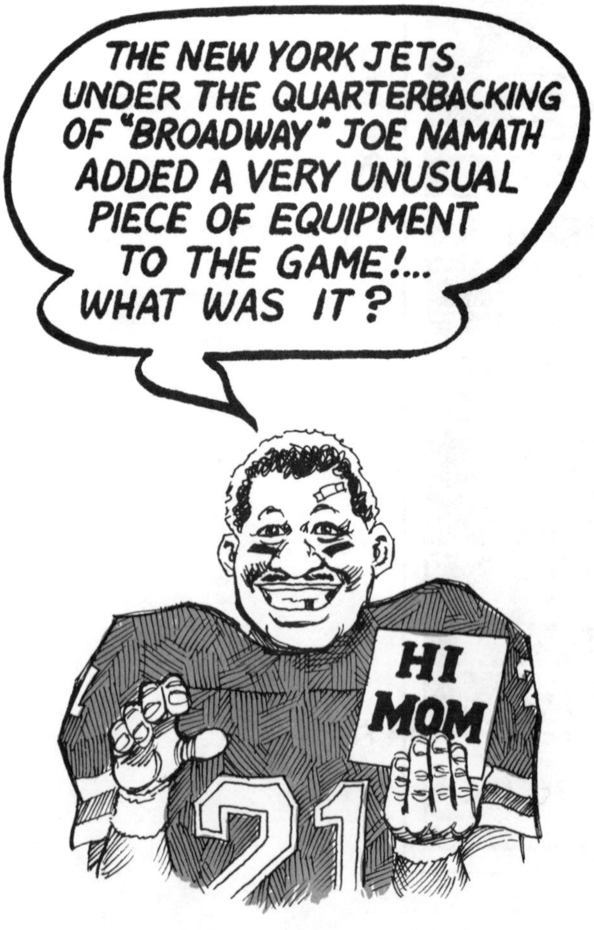

## BEFORE THE GAME

### Day 1

Day 1 is the day after the last game . . . the morning after . . . and most of the players feel that way. Today, though, they must re-live yesterday's game, witness all their mistakes in detail and hear about all their missed assignments.

The whole team, players and coaches, assemble for a 20 to 30 minute film of the game. The team in general is praised and/or criticized for their play.

Then the offense, defense, and specialty teams break off into separate meetings. At these smaller meetings, each player's activities on the field in the last game is gone over in detail — in front of everyone.

Also at these mini-meetings, the players are given "the book" on their next opponents. "The book" is an analysis of the types of plays their next opponents use, the frequency of their use, and in what situations they call which plays.

This provides the defense an indication of their opponent's tendencies. For example, what play do they most often call in a third down and long yardage situation? Knowing this information allows the defense to "anticipate" or be ahead of the offense.

"The book" also gives the players information about the opposing team's stars. How do they run? What's their most effective play? All the information needed if the defense is going to "shut the star down".

These films and meetings go a full day. That night the players go over and learn "the book" on their upcoming opponents.

★ ★ ★ ★ ★ TRIVIA ANSWER ★ ★ ★ ★ ★
★ PANTYHOSE! THAT'S RIGHT, PANTYHOSE. ★
★ THE EQUIPMENT MANAGER, BILL HAMPTON, ★
★ DECIDED THAT THE COLD WEATHER WAS ★
★ ADVERSLY AFFECTING THE PLAY OF SOME ★
★ OF HIS TEAM. AT FIRST MANY OF THE ★
★ PLAYERS LAUGHED AT THE IDEA OF WEARING ★
★ PANTYHOSE - BUT THE PANTYHOSE DID KEEP ★
★ THEM WARM, AND THEY DID WEAR THEM! ★
★ ★ ★ ★ ★ ★ ★ ★ ★ ★ ★ ★ ★ ★ ★ ★ ★ ★ ★

## Day 2

Today the team takes to the field to practice the things they learned from "the book" on their opponents. The team's offense pretends they are the opposing team and runs the opposing team's offense against their own team's defense.

In this way, the defense gets a chance to defend against the system they will face in the next game.

During this practice session, the defense alters its plays to match what they are now facing.

A major drawback to this session is that the stars on the offense of the opponent's team obviously are not there. It's hard to prepare a defense against stars.

AS A COACH, I'M CONCERNED ABOUT THE LITTLE THINGS THAT CAN GIVE MY TEAM AN EDGE: SUCH AS; A LINEMAN WHO CONSISTENTLY SIGNALS WHEN THE BALL IS GOING TO BE SNAPPED; DOES THE QUARTERBACK HAVE TROUBLE THROWING TO HIS OFFSIDE, i.e. WHEN HE'S MOVING AT RIGHT-ANGLES TO HIS THROWING DIRECTION; OR DOES ANY PLAYER APPEAR TO BE HIDING AN INJURY.

## Day 3

This day is very similar to day 2. The refinements in the defense become finer.

Today the team gets its own book for the next game. This book outlines the general game plan, specific new plays, special plays designed to be effective against the defense they are expecting and any new assignments.

Day 3 is the day to learn the book for the next game.

## Day 4

Today the team works on its own game plan on the field.

The second string offense runs the opponent's offense against the team's defense.

The second string defense defends against the team's offense as they run their new plays.

The whole day is taken in running and analysing the new offense and defense.

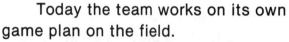

WHAT WAS THE ORIGINAL NAME OF THE NFL? WHEN THE ORIGINAL LEAGUE STARTED IN 1919, WHAT DID IT COST TO BUY A FRANCHISE?

## Day 5

This is the last day for any heavy workout on the field.

The coaches now must start considering the weather for game day and any injuries to their players that have not healed as fast as expected. The plays are altered one last time to account for weather and injuries.

Today, the last minute scouting reports on their opponents come in. These list any injuries they know about to opposing players, any new plays they have been running, and probable game plan changes they may have made. The team's tentative line up for the game is prepared.

If the team is playing away, today is the travel day.

★ ★ ★ TRIVIA ANSWER ★ ★ ★

ORIGINALLY, THE NFL WAS THE APFA, THE AMERICAN PROFESSIONAL FOOTBALL ASSOCIATION.

YOU COULD BUY A FRANCHISE IN 1919 FOR $25.00 (CASH!)

## Day 6

Today the team runs a light scrimmage on the opponent's playing field.

If they are playing at home, a light work out is scheduled. Their own field is being used by the opponents.

Also today, the weather conditions and players' health reports are updated.

The night of day 6 is an early one. No major meetings are held on day 6, but the coaches and players meet informally. Tension is very high on day 6.

# AMERICAN FOOTBALL

## GAME DAY — DAY 7

**8:00 A.M.:** The team has breakfast together. Usually the breakfast is designed to give the players "carbohydrate loading" — that is high in protein and carbohydrates. The meal probably consists of steaks and eggs, along with special high protein — high carbohydrate drinks.
Following breakfast many teams hold a prayer meeting which is usually led by one of the players.

**9:30 A.M.:** Those players requiring special needs leave for the stadium. Those special things may include difficult taping requirements (ribs, ankles), special medical preparations and any shots needed.

**10:00 A.M.:** All remaining players must leave for the stadium. usually the last bus leaves shortly after 10:00 a.m.

**11:00 A.M.:** All players begin suiting up.

**12:00 NOON:** The team takes a light workout on the field to loosen up and relieve some of the tensions.

**1:00 P.M.:** The team is back in their dressing room now. They change into their game uniforms and take care of any last minute equipment adjustments. Any sprains or cuts are worked on now.

There is a team meeting to finalize the game plan and discuss the field conditions. Any last minute play alterations are made now.
A few minutes before going back onto the field the team "juices" itself up with a good old fashioned team pep talk.

When the team hits the field, they are ready to play, so let's start the game!

16

## LET'S START THE GAME!

### Coin Toss

Within 3 minutes of the start of play, the two teams' captains (most teams have several) meet the referee at the center of the field for the coin toss. The visiting team calls the toss. The team that wins the toss decides to go on offense first (receive the kick-off) or defence (do the kick-off).

At the beginning of the second half of the game, the team that lost the toss gets the choice.

DECIDING WHETHER TO KICK-OFF (GO ON DEFENCE), OR TO RECEIVE (GO ON OFFENCE) DEPENDS ON MANY FACTORS! THE WIND... THE WEATHER... THE SUN... FIELD CONDITIONS... MY ASSESSMENT OF THEIR TEAM...

## KICK-OFF

Play is started by a kick-off

(i) at the beginning of each half of the game.

(ii) after each *point after* try.

(iii)after a field goal attempt.

The kick-off is made from the kicking team's 35 yard line and between in the inbound lines.

The kicker may place the ball in a tee, have another player hold it or drop-kick it himself.

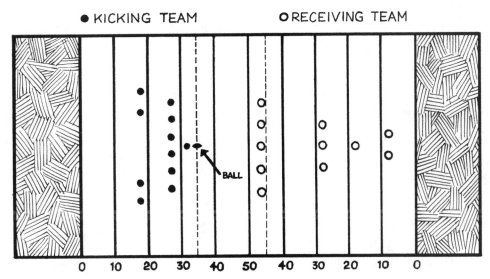

● KICKING TEAM      ○RECEIVING TEAM

BALL

0   10   20   30   40   50   40   30   20   10   0

RUNNING A KICK-OFF BACK FOR A TOUCHDOWN IS A DIFFICULT PLAY AND SELDOM ACCOMPLISHED. --ONE TEAM RAN BACK THE VERY FIRST KICK-OFF IT RECEIVED IN ITS VERY FIRST GAME. WHAT TEAM? WHO WAS THE BALL CARRIER?

## SPECIALTY TEAMS

A specialty team is a group of the team's players used mainly for one job — in this case the kick-off. The name usually given to the defensive line of the kicking team is the *suicide squad*, and for good reason. Here's the general thinking behind both the kicking team and the receiving team on a kick-off.

### Kicking Team

The kicker is not necessarily trying to kick the ball as far as he can. He does not want the ball to end up in his opponent's end zone. If it does, his opponents start play at their 20 yard line. Not distance, but height is what the kicker wants . . . height and placement.

Good height on a kick gives the ball a long hang time, that is, the higher the kick the longer it's in the air. This enables the kicking team to get downfield with the ball and be ready to tackle the receiver.

The suicide squad's job is to hurl themselves at the defensive wall and make it crumble thus exposing the receiver. Their assignment is to stop the ball carrier from running the ball back after it is caught.

### Coffin Corner

A great kick-off is one that goes high, drops away from a receiver, rolls to the corner of the playing field and stops on the one yard line.

*Coffin Corner* refers to either corner of the field at the one yard line.

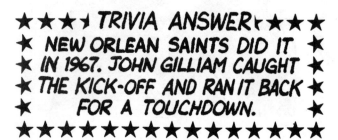

★★★★ TRIVIA ANSWER ★★★★
★ NEW ORLEAN SAINTS DID IT ★
★ IN 1967. JOHN GILLIAM CAUGHT ★
★ THE KICK-OFF AND RAN IT BACK ★
★ FOR A TOUCHDOWN. ★
★★★★★★★★★★★★★★★★★★★★

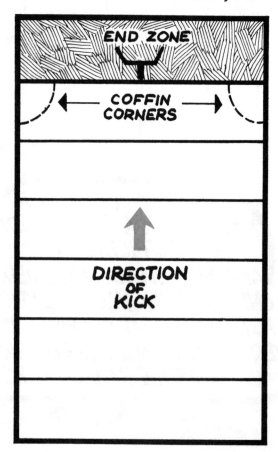

END ZONE

← COFFIN CORNERS →

↑

DIRECTION OF KICK

# AMERICAN FOOTBALL

## KICK-OFF RULES AND PENALTIES

**1.** All players of the kick-off team must be behind the ball at kick-off.

**2.** All players of the receiving team must be at least 10 yards away from the ball.

**3.** The kick-off must go at least 10 yards or a player on the receiving team must touch the ball.

**4.** No player may touch the kicker after the kick-off is completed, even accidentally while he is in the act of or just completing the kick. After the kick is completed, the kicker is just another player on the field and if he heads downfield into the play, he takes the same risks as a 280 pound lineman.

# AMERICAN FOOTBALL

## KICK-OFF PENALTIES

1. **ROUGHING THE KICKER:** no contact can be made with the kicker after the kick: 15 yards + 1st down

2. **RUNNING INTO THE KICKER:** unintentional contact with the kicker: 5 yards + 1st down

★★★★TRIVIA ANSWER★★★★
ERNIE WOOD OF THE
CANTON BULLDOGS - 1906

## KICK-OFF PENALTIES

**3. PLAYER ON KICKING TEAM DOWNFIELD:** players must be behind the ball at kick-off: 5 yards

**4. KICK-OFF OUT OF BOUNDS:** kick-off must stay inside the playing zone: kicking team re-kicks from 5 yards further back

## THE THREE KINDS OF KICKS USED FOR KICK-OFFS

1.  Kicking the ball off of a tee. This is the most common kick used at kick-off.

← KICKING TEE

2.  Having another player hold the ball in place. This is used on particularly windy days.

★★★TRIVIA ANSWER★★★
★ GREEN BAY PACKERS (35) ★
★ VS. KANSAS CITY CHIEFS (10). ★
★ WIDE RECEIVER, McGEE, FOR ★
★ THE PACKERS CAUGHT A 37 ★
★ YARD PASS FOR THE FIRST ★
★      TOUCHDOWN.      ★
★★★★★★★★★★★★★★★★★

**3. Using the Drop Kick:**

For a drop kick, the kicker drops the ball onto the playing surface and kicks it on the bounce.

This type of kick has not been used for years. It is unlikely you'll see it in a game.

THE DROP KICK IS HARDLY EVER USED TODAY. I HAVEN'T SEEN IT USED IN YEARS. I HOPE IT'S NOT TRUE, BUT THE REASON COMMONLY GIVEN FOR THE DEMISE OF THE DROP KICK IS THAT IT IS TOO HARD TO DO! - TAKES TOO MUCH SKILL!

# AMERICAN FOOTBALL

## KICK-OFF PLAYERS' POSITIONS

### Kicking Team

Every player on the kicking team must be behind the ball at the time of kick-off.

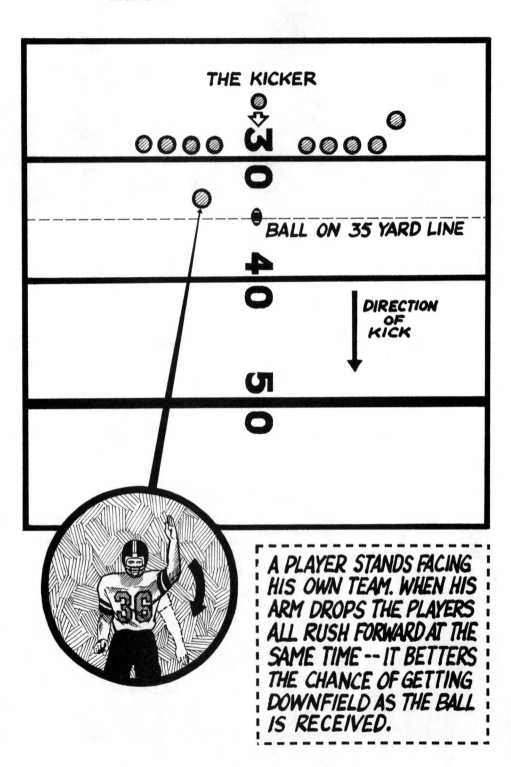

THE KICKER

BALL ON 35 YARD LINE

DIRECTION OF KICK

A PLAYER STANDS FACING HIS OWN TEAM. WHEN HIS ARM DROPS THE PLAYERS ALL RUSH FORWARD AT THE SAME TIME -- IT BETTERS THE CHANCE OF GETTING DOWNFIELD AS THE BALL IS RECEIVED.

# AMERICAN FOOTBALL

## Receiving Team

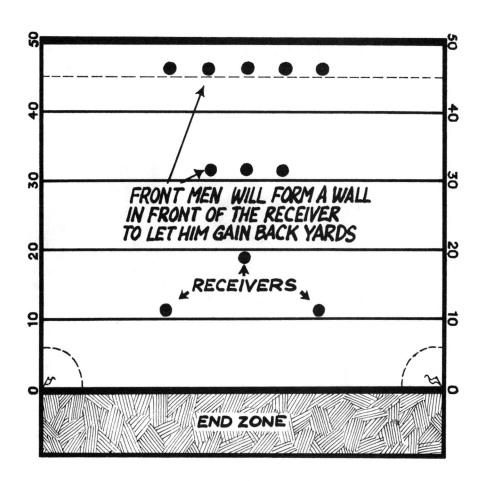

The receiving team's special unit is often made up of their second string defensive unit. Their job is to set up a wall to keep the kicking team's tacklers away from the ball carrier after he has caught the ball.

The receiving team, through its scouting reports, knows the way in which the kicker usually kicks the ball. The best ball returner on the receiving team tries to be where he predicts the kick will go.

No matter which player gets the ball, the defense immediately attempts to set up a protective wall of bodies for him. If the wall is set up well, the kick-off returner can run right downfield for a touchdown.

Of course it doesn't always work out that way.

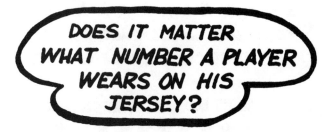

## The Receiver

The player receiving the kick-off has two options:

**1.** catch the ball and try to run back toward the other team's goal line as far as he can.

**2.** call for a *fair catch.* In this case, the offense starts at the point of the catch.

★★★★★★★★★★★★★★ *TRIVIA ANSWER* ★★★★★★★★★★★★★★

*YES! 1-19 QUARTERBACKS & KICKERS*    *20-49 RUNNING BACKS & DEFENSIVE BACKS*

*50-59 CENTERS & LINEBACKERS*    *60-79 INTERIOR OFFENSIVE LINEMEN & DEFENSIVE LINEMEN*

*80-89 WIDE RECEIVERS & TIGHT ENDS*    *90-99 DEFENSIVE LINEMEN*

## FAIR CATCH PENALTIES

HAND UP FOR FAIR CATCH →

BY TACKLING THE RECEIVER, THIS PLAYER GETS HIS TEAM A 15 YARD PENALTY

1. **Fair catch interference:** This occurs when the offense in any way obstructs the receiver after he has clearly made a fair catch signal: 15 yards.

2. **Moving forward after making a fair catch signal:** The receiver, after signalling for a fair catch, may only move two steps forward: 5 yards.

FAIR CATCH SIGNAL · BALL CAUGHT · 1 STEP · 2 STEPS · 3 STEPS (ILLEGAL) · 5 YARD PENALTY

I ADVISE MY RECEIVERS THAT ON ANY KICK-OFF, OR PUNT, IF YOU ARE GOING TO BE INSTANTLY HIT HARD ENOUGH TO PERHAPS HAVE A FUMBLE, CALL FOR A FAIR CATCH. THIS WILL OFTEN HAPPEN ON VERY HIGH KICKS, OR VERY SHORT KICKS -- IN BOTH THESE CASES THE PROTECTIVE WALL OF PLAYERS DOESN'T HAVE TIME TO FORM UP!

# AMERICAN FOOTBALL

## THE OFFENSE

### What are they trying to do?

The aim of the offense is to score points. To do that they must maintain possession of the ball. The offense gets four chances (downs) to move the ball 10 yards forward. If they do, they start at first down again and again have four downs to move the ball forward 10 yards. This continues until they score or fail to move the ball the required 10 yards.

FOOTBALL IS TRULY A TEAM SPORT- EVERY PLAYER MUST DO HIS JOB WELL IN ORDER FOR THE TEAM TO SCORE. EVERY OFFENSIVE PLAY DETAILS PRECISELY WHERE EACH PLAYER MUST GO, AND WHAT HIS SPECIFIC ASSIGNMENT IS.

WHICH FOOTBALL GREAT PLAYED IN THE NFL IN FOUR SUCCESSIVE DECADES ?

# AMERICAN FOOTBALL
## THE OFFENSE

The team receiving the ball goes on offense. They attempt to move the ball into the opposing team's end zone for points. The two most common ways for teams to score points are:

**1. Touchdown:** to score a touchdown, 6 points, the team must get the ball into the opponent's end zone and maintain possession of the ball. For example, a player, holding the ball, may run (fall, dive, leap, plunge, rush) into the end zone for a touchdown. Or, a player may catch a pass in the end zone which is also a touchdown.

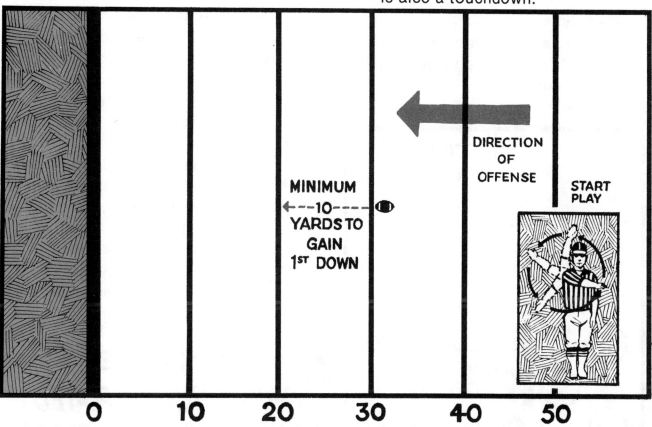

MINIMUM
← --10--- ◖
YARDS TO
GAIN
1ST DOWN

DIRECTION
OF
OFFENSE

START
PLAY

0      10      20      30      40      50

**2. Field Goal:** to score a field goal, 3 points, the team must place kick the ball from behind the line of scrimmage, through the opponent's uprights and above the crossbar.

IF MY TEAM IS IN THE OPPONENT'S END OF THE FIELD, AND IT'S THE FOURTH DOWN, OR THERE'S ONLY ENOUGH TIME LEFT FOR ONE PLAY, I'LL CALL FOR A FIELD GOAL ATTEMPT. THE KICKER WILL KICK FROM ABOUT 10 YARDS BEHIND THE LINE OF SCRIMMAGE. SO IF THE PLAY STARTS ON THEIR 30 YARD LINE, THE FIELD GOAL TRY WILL ACTUALLY BE ABOUT A 40 YARD ATTEMPT.

## THE OFFENSE

**Center:** This is the player in the center of the offensive line. There are three linemen on either side of him on the line of scrimmage.

His main responsibility is to ensure a good, clean snap of the ball. He knows the instant he starts moving the football, he's going to be hit by the opposing linemen.

He must snap the ball and come up blocking as a key interior lineman. Center is a very tough position to play on the line.

**Guards:** There are two guards, one on each side of the center, a left guard and a right guard. Their basic assignment is blocking but where and how they block depends on the play being run.

On running plays designed to take the ball carrier around the end of the line, that is on sweeps, the guards start on the line as always. As the ball is snapped, they drop back off the line and become lead blockers for the ball carrier. That is, they run in front of the runner, blocking opponents from tackling the ball carrier.

On running plays designed to take the ball carrier through the line, interior running plays, the guards start and stay on the line. They must block and break up any defensive pattern they face. Guards must be strong, quick and flexible in their thinking.

SCRIMMAGE
◆ LINE

LEFT GUARD

CENTER

RIGHT GUARD

★★★★TRIVIA ANSWER ★★★★
GEORGE BLANDA PLAYED
FOR THE CHICAGO BEARS
FROM 1949 TO 1958,
THE HOUSTON OILERS FROM
1960 TO 1966 AND THE
OAKLAND RAIDERS FROM
1967 TO 1976

# AMERICAN FOOTBALL
## THE OFFENSE

**Tackles:** There are two tackles, one on each side of the guards, a left tackle and a right tackle. They are heavy duty blockers. They must stop any opponents from getting through their line. They must be big, tough and strong.

**Ends:** Again, there are two ends, a left end and a right end.
If he is right next to a tackle, the player is called the tight end.
If he is moved away to the right or left from the tackle, he is called a split end. These players are often ball handlers. They can become eligible pass receivers. Or they can be ball carriers on several different types of running plays.

AN NFL TEAM HAS 45 PLAYERS ON ITS ROSTER. USUALLY THEY BREAK DOWN THIS WAY: OFFENSIVE LINEMEN: 8 RECEIVERS: 6 RUNNING BACKS: 5 QUARTERBACKS: 3 DEFENSIVE LINEMEN: 6 LINEBACKERS: 8 DEFENSIVE BACKS: 7 KICKER: 1 PUNTER: 1

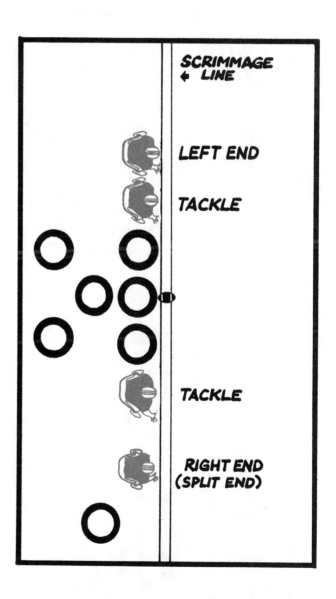

SCRIMMAGE LINE

LEFT END

TACKLE

TACKLE

RIGHT END (SPLIT END)

# AMERICAN FOOTBALL
## THE OFFENSE

**Half Backs:** There are usually two half backs in the backfield. They are the speedsters on the team. They are involved in many running plays but as well they are good pass receivers.

They form part of the defensive horseshoe that sets up around the quarterback on some passing plays (the pocket).

*FOOTBALL IS CERTAINLY VIOLENT!-BUT WAS THERE EVER A TIME WHEN AN AMERICAN PRESIDENT THREATENED TO BAN FOOTBALL BECAUSE IT WAS TOO BRUTAL?*

**Running Backs or Full Backs:** This player usually lines up behind everyone else. He will be used mainly on running plays.

The running back is like a freight train, able to move straight ahead and carry most of the opposing team on his back while he's doing it. As well as great strength, the running back must have agility, be able to change directions, and have an uncanny sense of balance. He wants to be able to move low and fast but stay on his feet as long as possible.

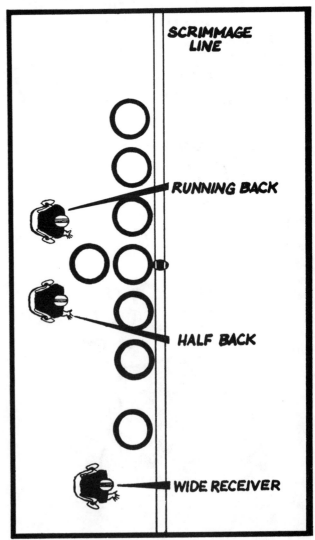

# AMERICAN FOOTBALL
## THE OFFENSE

**Quarterback:** The quarterback is the field marshal. He's in charge on the field. He's the leader of the team and must be able to command the respect of the other players.

In the huddle, he will inform the others of what play they are running.

When he moves the team to the line of scrimmage, he looks the defensive alignment over. Now he has three choices.

1. If he likes the defense he is facing, he will put the ball into play just as called for in the huddle. No changes.

2. If he sees something he thinks is a weakness or a particular problem in the defense, he can call a check-off. This is changing one part of the play, perhaps the direction of the run or the timing of the snap. He uses a code word or number to tell his team he has made a change and what the change is.

3. If he sees a totally unexpected defense, the quarterback can call an audible. That is he changes the play at the line of scrimmage. Again, he uses special codes to let his team know what the new play is.

The quarterback gets the ball on the snap. He is the beginning point of all plays. He must be a great athlete.

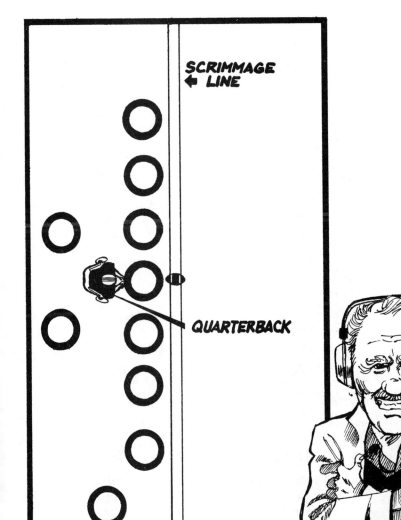

SCRIMMAGE LINE

QUARTERBACK

A SIMPLE SORE THROAT IS ONLY AN INCONVENIENCE TO MOST PEOPLE, BUT TO A QUARTERBACK IT'S A SERIOUS INJURY. IF THE Q.B. CAN'T "BARK" OUT THOSE COMMANDS ON THE LINE LOUD ENOUGH TO BE HEARD OVER THE ROAR OF THE CROWD, HE CAN'T GO INTO THE GAME.

## THE LINE OF SCRIMMAGE

The line of scrimmage is an imaginary line passing through the end of the ball closest to your team's goal line. There are really two lines of scrimmage, one for each team. The space between them is the neutral zone.

It's in the neutral zone that much of the game's battle takes place. Here's where the half ton of the defensive front four meets the onrushing offensive line. Heads crash, bodies bash bodies, each player intent on completing his assignment. The term "neutral zone" is a great misnomer.

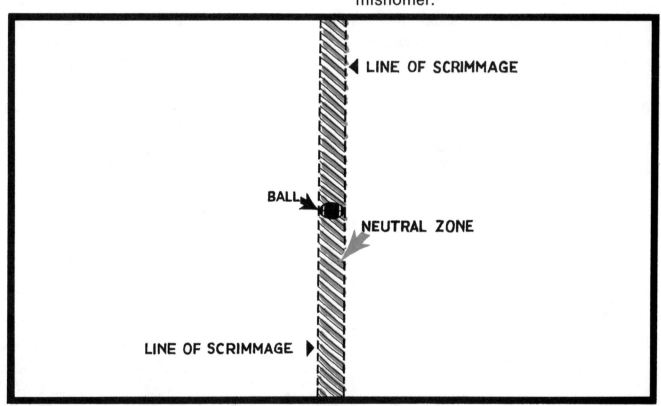

LINE OF SCRIMMAGE

BALL

NEUTRAL ZONE

LINE OF SCRIMMAGE

★★★★★★★★★★★ TRIVIA ANSWER ★★★★★★★★★★★★★★
★ AT THE END OF THE 1905 SEASON, SEVERAL UNIVERSITIES DROPPED FOOTBALL-THEY ★
★ SAID IT WAS THE BRUTALITY (IT WAS PROBABLY THE HIGH COSTS OF RUNNING A
★ FOOTBALL TEAM). THAT YEAR 15 PLAYERS DIED IN GAMES. PRESIDENT THEODORE ★
★ ROOSEVELT DESCRIBED THE GAME AS "...WASTEFUL, WANTON BARBARITY." HE ★
★ THREATENED TO MAKE THE GAME ILLEGAL IF CHANGES WEREN'T INSTITUTED. ★
★ THOSE CHANGES MADE THE GAME SAFER, LESS BRUTAL, AND MOST IMPORTANT, ★
★        KEPT FOOTBALL A LEGAL GAME.                                    ★
★★★★★★★★★★★★★★★★★★★★★★★★★★★★★★★★★

# AMERICAN FOOTBALL

35 above.

## THE LINE OF SCRIMMAGE

The team on offense must put at least seven men at the line of scrimmage to start a down. The other offensive players must be at least one yard behind the line (except the player who will receive the snap).

Another exception ... the center, the player who will snap the ball, is allowed to lean into the neutral zone ... but not across the opposing line of scrimmage.

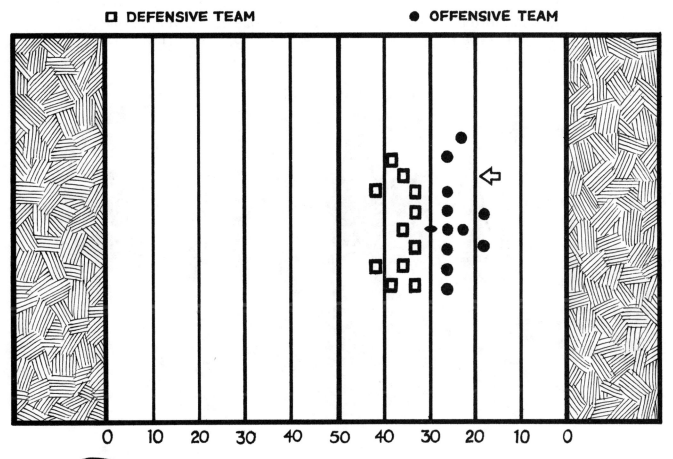

□ DEFENSIVE TEAM    ● OFFENSIVE TEAM

WHY DOES THE COACH BOTHER USING PLAYERS TO CARRY IN HIS PLAYS TO THE QUARTERBACK WHEN HE COULD SIMPLY PUT A RADIO RECEIVER IN HIS QUARTERBACK'S HELMET AND RADIO THE PLAYS IN?

# AMERICAN FOOTBALL
## THE HUDDLE

Before each down, the offense goes into a huddle — a team meeting on the field. The quarterback tells his team the play for that down. He will tell them who gets the ball, whether it's a run or pass, when the ball will be snapped, what side of the line the play will move to — all the details but in a code so all the information is given quickly and secretly.

The quarterback in the past used to call all the plays for the team. He would decide what he thought would be best to try in that particular situation. In today's game, it is rare to find a coach that allows his quarterback that kind of decision making on the field. The coach usually sends in each play. The quarterback must execute the play.

When the huddle starts, the official indicates that the timer be started — a large electronic clock on the field. The offense is given 30 seconds to get the ball into play.

★★★★★★★★★★★★★ **TRIVIA ANSWER** ★★★★★★★★★★★★★

IN 1957, PAUL BROWN, THE HIGHLY SUCCESSFUL COACH OF THE CLEVELAND BROWNS GAVE HIS QUARTERBACK A RADIO-EQUIPPED HELMET. THE OPPOSING TEAM, THE DETROIT LIONS, ATTEMPTED TO SMASH THE HELMET: THEY PUNCHED AT IT, KICKED IT, HIT IT WITH THEIR OWN HELMETS. THEN ONE PLAYER ON THE DETROIT TEAM GOT A RADIO RECEIVER OF THEIR OWN AND STARTED TUNING INTO THE SIGNALS BEING SENT OUT BY THE BROWNS. DETROIT CLAIMED THEY KNEW EVERY PLAY THE BROWNS TRIED IN THE SECOND HALF. DETROIT WON THE GAME 21 – 9. IT IS NOW ILLEGAL TO USE RADIO OR ELECTRONIC DEVICES IN THE GAME.

# AMERICAN FOOTBALL

## OFFENSIVE LINE FORMATIONS

### The Pro Set

This formation is a standard offensive line set. The two running backs (halfback and fullback) line up behind the quarterback. The third back is set off as a flanker, in this case a flanker left (split end).

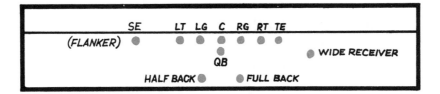

### I Formation

In this formation, the running backs line up in a straight line behind the quarterback. The center, quarterback and running backs form the letter I. This formation is good for running plays. A good running back has time to see where a hole in the line is opening up and head into it.

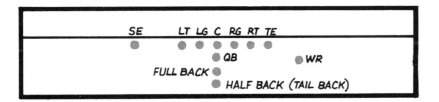

## THE HOLE NUMBERS

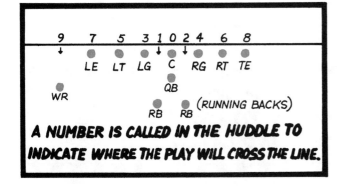

A NUMBER IS CALLED IN THE HUDDLE TO INDICATE WHERE THE PLAY WILL CROSS THE LINE.

HAS A PLAYER EVER DIED IN PRO-FOOTBALL?

## OFFENSIVE LINE FORMATIONS

### Slot Formation

In the slot formation, two wide receivers go to one side, here we've shown them on the right. The tight end plays the opposite side of the formation. The backs can be in several positions. Here we've shown them in an *I* set up.

A slot formation is when the wide receiver lines up in the slot between the tackle and the split end on the weak side and a yard behind the line. This receiver is then called a *slot back.*

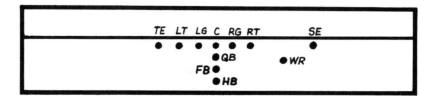

### Split

In the split formation, the running backs are split on either side of the quarterback. This formation is good for rushing plays. One back leads the other through the line. Plays from this formation often run to the strong side, in this diagram, that's the right.

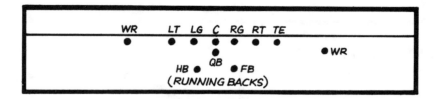

# AMERICAN FOOTBALL

## OFFENSIVE LINE FORMATIONS

### Opposite

In this formation, the halfback splits to the weak side while the fullback is directly behind the quarterback. This formation is often used on running plays to the weak side, in our diagram, that's the left.

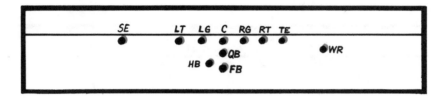

### Near

This formation is the flip side of the *opposite.* Here the halfback splits to the strong side (right). In this formation the right tackle, tight end and halfback can all block for the fullback. This is used often when the team needs a yard or so (short yardage) for a first down or a touchdown.

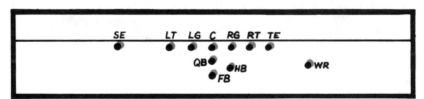

ONLY ONE FRANCHISE EVER WON ITS LEAGUE CHAMPIONSHIP IN ITS FIRST YEAR OF PLAY. NAME THE TEAM.

## OFFENSIVE LINE FORMATIONS

### Shotgun

The shotgun is primarily a passing formation. The quarterback takes the snap standing about five yards back. He is instantly ready to pass. He has five receivers quickly downfield. In this set up, even the quarterback is an eligible reciever.

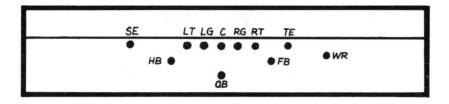

MY QUARTERBACK MAY CALL FOR THIS FORMATION AFTER HE LOOKS AT THE DEFENSE. IF HE FEELS THEY ARE SET FOR A BIG PASS RUSH (A BLITZ) HE CALLS A NEW SET OF NUMBERS (AN AUDIBLE) TO TELL HIS TEAM THE NEW PLAY. IT IS OFTEN A VERY EFFECTIVE MOVE AGAINST THE PASS RUSH!

★★★★★ TRIVIA ANSWER ★★★★★★★★
★ THE CLEVELAND BROWNS : 1950 WAS
★ THEIR FIRST YEAR IN THE NFL. THEY
★ DEFEATED THE LOS ANGELES RAMS
★ 30 TO 28 FOR THE CHAMPIONSHIP.
★★★★★★★★★★★★★★★★★★★★★★

# AMERICAN FOOTBALL

## Blocking

To make a running play a success, the blockers must complete their assignments. One may be to create a hole in the defensive line, that is, move the defensive linemen out of the way so the offensive back can run through.

Another assignment is called, *lead blocking.* In this type of blocking, two or more offensive linemen or other backs, run in front of the ball carrier. They *lead* the runner downfield, blocking the defensive along the way, thus clearing a path for the runner.

A third blocking assignment is blocking downfield before the ball carrier reaches the area. When the runner does arrive, the defense is neutralized.

To understand how important the blockers on the line are, consider:

In 1973, O.J. Simpson set a new record for yards gained rushing, 2,003, in one season. At the press conference, O.J. had all his offensive linemen with him to accept the award.

In 1977, William Payton led the league in rushing. He gave expensive wrist watches to each of his offensive linemen.

In a running play, the blockers must complete their assignments — and it doesn't matter if they exhibit less than perfect form — as long as they give the ball carrier some running room.

## Blocking Patterns

**Angle:** linemen block on a slant right or left

**Double Team:** two on one blocking

**Wedge:** three on one blocking

**Gross Block:** a scissor like exchange of blocking assignments by two offensive linemen

**Lead Blocking:** a running back blocking in front of another back

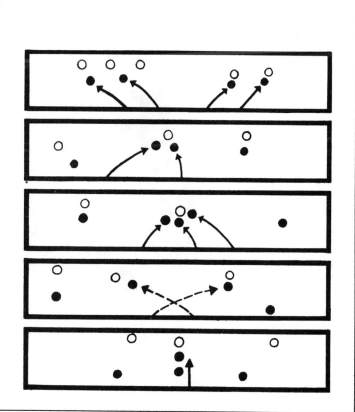

**Blocking:** A player may use the upper part of his body to obstruct an opponent.

The blocker may not lock his hands together or punch or slap the opponent.

The blocker's hands must be completely or semi-closed.

A player may block an opponent at any time so long as it doesn't cause pass interference or interfere with a pass reception, a fair catch, a kicker or a passer.

BODY BLOCK

## Interesting Exceptions

1. **The Straight Arm:** The ball carrier may use his hand to push a potential tackler out of his way. This technique is called a straight arm or stiff arm.

2. **Body Block:** When putting a body block on an opponent, the blocker does not have to keep his hands closed and in contact with his body.

STRAIGHT ARM

## ILLEGAL BLOCKS

INTERLOCKING OPPOSING PLAYER'S ARM

**1. Arm Interlocking:**
This type of blocking brings a 15 yard penalty.

TWO BLOCKERS WITH ARMS INTERLOCKED

HANDS INTERLOCKED

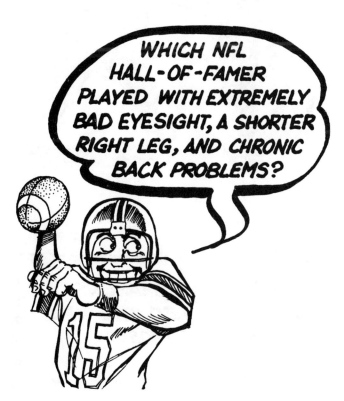

WHICH NFL HALL-OF-FAMER PLAYED WITH EXTREMELY BAD EYESIGHT, A SHORTER RIGHT LEG, AND CHRONIC BACK PROBLEMS?

## ILLEGAL BLOCKS

2. **Spearing:** A blocker may not drive his helmet into an opposing player. Spearing is penalized as unsportsmanlike conduct. 15 yard penalty

**SPEARING**

### TRIPPING

3. **Tripping:** 15 yard penalty

### FACE MASK

4. **Face Mask:** A blocker (or anyone else) may not grab an opponent's face mask. It is also illegal to poke your fingers into your opponent's eyes.   15 yard penalty

★★★★★★★★★★★★★TRIVIA ANSWER★★★★★★★★★★★★★★★

RAYMOND BERRY NOT ONLY PLAYED FOR 12 SEASONS WITH THE BALTIMORE COLTS, BUT HE ALSO LED THE NFL IN TOTAL PASS RECEPTIONS FOR THREE OF THOSE SEASONS.

# AMERICAN FOOTBALL

## THE FORWARD PASS

This is a pass thrown from inside or behind the neutral zone downfield toward the opponent's goal line. The passer spins the ball as he throws to cause the ball to rotate or spiral smoothly in order to cut down wind resistance and give the pass greater accuracy.

For the pass to be complete, termed a completion, completed pass or a reception, it must be caught before touching the ground by an eligible receiver who remains in bounds until he has demonstrated control of the ball.

If the receiver is tackled while he is in the air catching the ball and is driven out of bounds, and the referee judges the receiver would have landed in bounds if he had not been tackled, the catch is deemed a completion.

### Who Is An Eligible Receiver?

Basically, there are five players legally able to run downfield and catch a forward pass; the two ends and any player in the backfield who is one yard behind the line of scrimmage at the time of the snap.

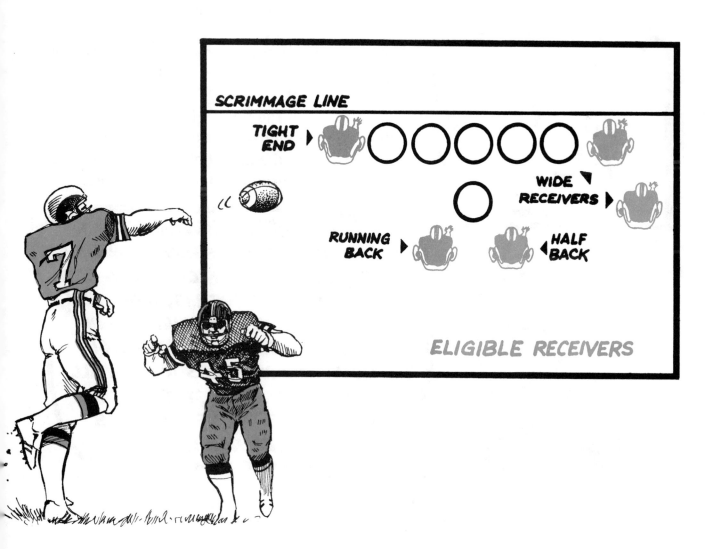

## MOVING THE BALL FORWARD

From the time the official signals the clock to start for a series of downs, the offense has just 30 seconds to get the ball into play.

The offense has four downs to move the ball forward 10 yards. If it is successful, they get 4 more downs. This continues until the offense scores or they fail to advance the ball 10 yards.

If the offense fails to get 10 yards, the opposing team gets possession of the ball at the point where the officials whistle it dead.

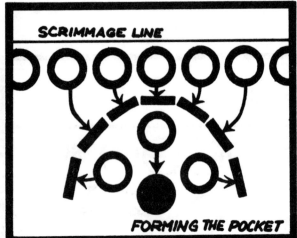

SCRIMMAGE LINE

FORMING THE POCKET

## THE POCKET

The quarterback requires time to throw a forward pass: time to get set, time to allow his receivers to get downfield, time to cock his arm and throw. The defense tries very hard to rush the passer or better to tackle him before he can throw and maybe cause him to fumble the ball.

The quarterback drops back and a protective wall made up of the other backs and the five interior linemen forms in a horseshoe shape around him. The area inside this protective semi-circle is called the pocket.

A good pocket should give the passer about three seconds: any more is a gift, any less and the play is in trouble.

If the pocket breaks down, that is the defense breaks through, the quarterback can of course run to get away from the defensive players.

IN PRACTICE, THE QUARTERBACK AND HIS RECEIVERS RUN THE PASS PLAYS SO THE QUARTERBACK CAN LEARN HOW FAST EACH RECEIVER IS, HOW THEY RUN THEIR PATTERNS, WHAT SIDE OF THEIR BODIES THEY CATCH PASSES ON. THE QUARTERBACK NEEDS TO KNOW ALL THIS BECAUSE HE MUST THROW THE BALL WHERE THE RECEIVER IS "GOING TO BE," NOT WHERE HE IS.

## PASSING PLAYS

### FORWARD PASS PATTERNS

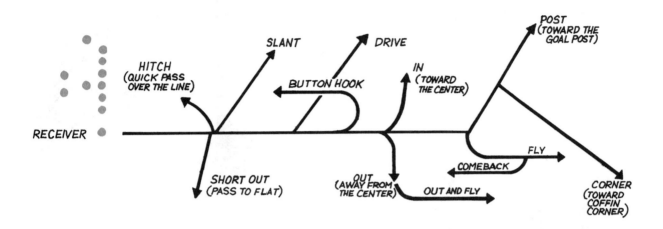

The offense has many different ways of moving the ball forward. They can use running plays (discussed later on) that go directly through the defense or around the end of the defensive line. They can try passing the ball (discussed later on) downfield to gain yards against the defense. Or they can use combinations of those two play types.

The neutral zone, that space between the two opposing zones, is also known as the pit, or the trenches, or the war zone. As you can tell from its various names, this area sees the action. It's in the trenches that games are won and lost. The team that can dominate the line can usually win the game.

THESE PASS PATTERNS FORM THE BASIS ON WHICH A GOOD RECEIVER AND CALM QUARTERBACK BUILD A WHOLE SYSTEM THAT REALLY IS TOTALLY UNDERSTOOD ONLY BY THEM. THE QUARTERBACK AND HIS RECEIVERS DEVELOP ALMOST A "SECOND NATURE" UNDERSTANDING OF EACH OTHER'S TIMING AND LIKELY MOVES.

## PENALTIES

**Illegal Forward Pass:** The passer goes over the line of scrimmage before throwing the pass: 5 yards + loss of down.

**Ineligible Player Downfield:** Any player other than an end or back downfield on a passing play: 10 yards.

**Second Forward Pass:** The offense tries a second forward pass in the same play: loss of down.

# AMERICAN FOOTBALL
## PASSING PENALTIES

If the forward pass is successful, that is a legal receiver catches the ball, the next play begins where that receiver is stopped by the defense.

To be successful, the pass must be caught in bounds. The receiver must show possession of the ball and have both feet touch down in bounds for a pass to be judged complete. It's not where the receiver starts to catch the ball but where he ends up with the ball that is the deciding factor. Possession is a judgement call by the official but usually it means in the receiver's hands and not being jiggled or bounced.

If the passer drops the ball before he passes it, the ball is ruled fumbled and not an incomplete pass. The difference is important. On an incomplete forward pass, the ball is dead and the offense retains possession. But on a fumble, the ball is still in play and may be picked up and moved by any player on either team.

Not often seen, but in the rule books, is the situation where two eligible receivers catch the ball together. It is ruled an incomplete forward pass.

**Unusual Situations:**

1.  Forward pass is thrown on the fourth down into the opponent's end zone from a line of scrimmage inside their 20 yard line and is incomplete. The ball is placed back at the 20 yard line for start of play by the opposing team.

2.  A foul is committed by the offense prior to the pass being completed. The play is called back even if the pass is completed to the point of the foul from where the penalized yards are marched off.

3.  The receiver catches the ball in the air over the playing field but is tackled at the same time and driven out of bounds before he lands. This pass is complete since the tackle took the receiver out of bounds. The next down starts at the point at which he went out.

# AMERICAN FOOTBALL

## PENALTIES ON THE FORWARD PASS

### 1. In-and-out-of-bounds

The receiver cannot run out of bounds then come back onto the playing field and catch a pass. Once out of bounds, he is no longer an eligible receiver.

### 2. Landing in bounds

Landing in bounds means bringing both feet down onto the playing field while in possession of the ball.
If the receiver's momentum while he leaps up to catch the ball carries him out of bounds, the pass is incomplete.

## PENALTIES ON THE FORWARD PASS

### 3. Simultaneous catching of the ball

If the receiver and one of the defending players catch the ball together, the pass is ruled complete and the receiver maintains possession.

### 4. Possession of the ball

In the rules, possession is having enough control of the ball to initiate an action that is part of the game. Such an action may be simply falling after making a catch, or taking a step, or preparing to run. Normally it is easy to decide whether a player has possession or not.
But on those borderline cases, the judgement of the nearest official is the deciding factor. It becomes a judgement call.

WHO IS CREDITED WITH CATCHING THE FIRST FORWARD PASS THROWN IN A PROFESSIONAL FOOTBALL GAME?

## PENALTIES ON THE FORWARD PASS

### 5. What if the ball hits another player?

If a forward pass touches an ineligible receiver, even accidently, the forward pass cannot be completed, even if it is eventually caught by an eligible player.
A defensive player may hit or bat the ball at any time during a forward pass play. The defenders can direct the ball through a hit or a slap. The offense, though, may only bat the ball in order to stop a defensive player from getting it.

### 6. Intentional grounding

The quarterback has the snapped ball but doesn't have time to throw the pass or none of his eligible receivers are in the clear (no defenders around). He sees the defense coming at him. If they tackle him (sacking the quarterback), the quarterback's team will have lost a lot of yardage. If, on the other hand, the quarterback can throw a pass at "no one", but just to get the pass thrown, he is intentionally grounding the ball. The penalty is 5 yards and loss of down.
It is not often easy for the officials to make this call. Was it intentional grounding or just a bad throw made by a quarterback under a lot of pressure?

★★★★ TRIVIA ANSWER ★★★
EDDIE WOOD, PLAYING
FOR THE
CANTON BULLDOGS
IN 1906.

## PASSING PLAYS

The forward pass is an essential element to a successful offense. But to make the forward pass a powerful weapon, the offense must be able to run the ball as well. The offense must use dozens of different plays and formations in an effort to confound and confuse the defense.

### Play-Action Pass

In order to confuse the defense, on this type of play, the quarterback fakes (pretends) to hand the ball off to one of his backs. This fake ball carrier then follows his lead blockers into the line. They take as many of the defense with them as possible.

In the meantime, the quarterback, who has kept the ball out of sight by riding it on his hip, drops back to pass.

The whole point of this deception is to delay the pass rush by the defense and to make the pass defenders start in toward the line. The offense only needs a split second advantage to get a really good play to click.

The play-action pass is a good call on second or third downs with short yardage to go. The defense cannot be sure you won't run so they are more likely to commit to a fake run.

QUARTERBACK SPINS TO BACK

QUARTERBACK EXECUTES FAKE

BACK DRAWS OFF OPPOSITION

SCRAMBLING IS A TERM TO DESCRIBE THE RUNNING A QUARTERBACK MUST DO TO ELUDE DEFENDERS WHO HAVE BROKEN THROUGH THE OFFENSIVE LINE.

## PASSING PLAYS

### Screen Pass

This play is used when the defense has been rushing the quarterback effectively. The screen is designed to use the rushing defense as part of the offensive play.

The quarterback drops back to pass. The offensive linemen don't block quite as hard as usual. The defensive line breaks through and rushes at the quarterback. Suddenly a receiver moves into the flat and the quarterback unloads a pass just over the heads of the rushing defenders. The offensive linemen meanwhile have moved over to block for the receiver.

The quarterback, to keep the downfield defenders downfield and out of the play, will often pump his arm once or twice as though he intends to throw a long pass.

A further advantage of the screen is that the quarterback can still throw long if he sees one of his downfield receivers is open.

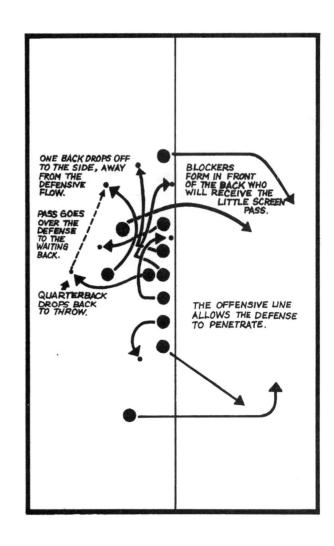

ONE BACK DROPS OFF TO THE SIDE, AWAY FROM THE DEFENSIVE FLOW.

PASS GOES OVER THE DEFENSE TO THE WAITING BACK.

QUARTERBACK DROPS BACK TO THROW.

BLOCKERS FORM IN FRONT OF THE BACK WHO WILL RECEIVE THE LITTLE SCREEN PASS.

THE OFFENSIVE LINE ALLOWS THE DEFENSE TO PENETRATE.

ON PASSING PLAYS, INTERIOR LINEMEN ARE NOT ALLOWED MORE THAN ONE YARD DOWNFIELD FROM THE LINE OF SCRIMMAGE BEFORE THE BALL IS THROWN.

# AMERICAN FOOTBALL

## PASSING PLAYS

**Lateral Pass:** A ball passed backward or on a line parallel to the line of scrimmage. This pass may be thrown at any time. Any player on either team may throw or receive this pass.

If the ball touches the ground while a lateral pass is being executed, the defensive team can recover it and take possession but may not advance it. The offensive team may recover and move a dropped lateral pass.

WHY WAS SUPER BOWL III A VERY IMPORTANT GAME?

## RUNNING PLAYS

### Traps

A trap play is another deception used by the offense, this time by the offensive line. Tackles and centers may execute a trap, but most often it is done by the guards.

In a trap play, the offensive lineman who is the "hole" that the runner is going to go through, pulls away from the line rather than block forward. The defender facing him moves into the space left and is immediately hit by another offensive lineman pulling away from a different point on the line.

A successful trap depends entirely on the quickness, perfect timing and teamwork of the offensive linemen.

OFFENSIVE LINEMAN PULLS AWAY FROM THE LINE TO LURE THE DEFENDER FACING HIM INTO HIS SPACE

AN OFFENSIVE LINEMAN FROM THE OPPOSITE SIDE RUNS INTO THE DEFENDER IN THE HOLE

THE OFFENSIVE LINEMAN WHO OPENED THE HOLE THEN SLANTS INTO THE MIDDLE CLEARING A PATH FOR THE BALL CARRIER

### Sweeps

This is a general term for running plays that go around the end of the line. The ball carrier sweeps wide of the tight end behind lead blockers. If the blockers can spring the runner, sweeps can be great yard gainers.

THE BALL CARRIER RUNS ALONG BEHIND HIS BLOCKERS READY TO BREAK OUT INTO THE OPEN.

★★★★ TRIVIA ANSWER ★★★★
THE COLTS WERE HEAVY FAVORITES TO DESTROY THE JETS. JOE NAMATH LED THE JETS TO VICTORY: 16 -7. THIS VICTORY WAS IMPORTANT IN THAT IT GAVE CREDIBILITY TO THE AFC.

## RUNNING PLAYS

### The Draw Play

This play is the opposite of the play-action pass. Here the offense wants the defense to believe that a pass play is being set up. The offense lines up in a passing formation. The receivers start downfield after the snap. All the blocking assignments begin as pass blocking. The quarterback drops back as if to pass.

The point of all this deception is to lure the defense into a pass rush. Then when they have committed, the quarterback suddenly hands the ball off to one of his backs and the defense is facing a running play.

The draw play works well if the defense is expecting a pass, such as late in the game and the offense is behind and they are within striking distance. The defense will expect, in this situation, that the offense will try for a touchdown pass.

The draw play is also effective when the defense has been charging a lot on its own. The draw uses the defense against itself.

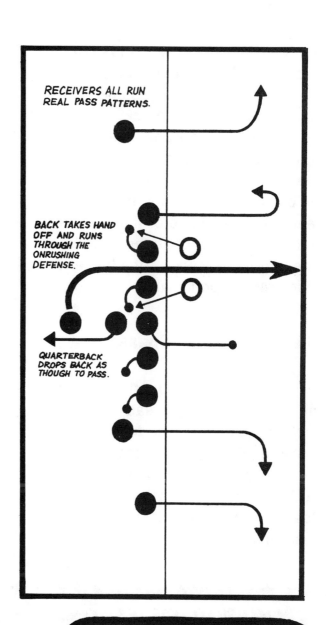

RECEIVERS ALL RUN REAL PASS PATTERNS.

BACK TAKES HAND OFF AND RUNS THROUGH THE ONRUSHING DEFENSE.

QUARTERBACK DROPS BACK AS THOUGH TO PASS.

A PLAYER RAN 66 YARDS FOR A TOUCHDOWN, BUT INSTEAD OF GAINING 6 POINTS FOR HIS TEAM, THE OPPONENTS GOT 2 POINTS! WHAT HAPPENED?

# AMERICAN FOOTBALL

## RUNNING PLAYS

### The Quarterback Keeper

When the offense is close to their opponent's goal line, the defense gets heavy in the center of the line. This makes them open to quick runs around the end or short passes. In a quarterback keeper play, the quarterback fakes a hand off to one of his backs. The back and his blockers head into the middle of the line. The quarterback then bootlegs (runs to one side) around the end of the line and heads for a touchdown.

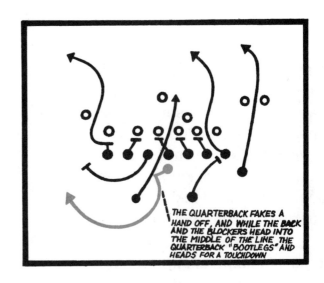

THE QUARTERBACK FAKES A HAND OFF, AND WHILE THE BACK AND THE BLOCKERS HEAD INTO THE MIDDLE OF THE LINE THE QUARTERBACK "BOOTLEGS" AND HEADS FOR A TOUCHDOWN

### The Quarterback Sneak

In this play, the quarterback takes the snap and then instead of dropping back or handing off, he follows his center right into the defensive line.

This play is used on very short yardage and not too often even then. Coaches do not like risking injury to their quarterbacks.

FROM THE SNAP THE QUARTERBACK CHARGES UP THROUGH THE DEFENSIVE LINE BEHIND HIS CENTER.

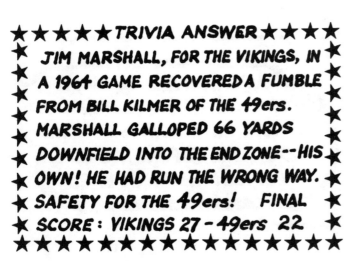

★★★★★TRIVIA ANSWER★★★★
★ JIM MARSHALL, FOR THE VIKINGS, IN ★
★ A 1964 GAME RECOVERED A FUMBLE ★
★ FROM BILL KILMER OF THE 49ers. ★
★ MARSHALL GALLOPED 66 YARDS ★
★ DOWNFIELD INTO THE END ZONE--HIS ★
★ OWN! HE HAD RUN THE WRONG WAY. ★
★ SAFETY FOR THE 49ers!   FINAL ★
★ SCORE: VIKINGS 27 - 49ers 22 ★
★★★★★★★★★★★★★★★★★★★

# AMERICAN FOOTBALL

## THE OFFICIALS

**REFEREE:** The referee is the chief official and has over-all responsibility for the game. As well, his specific duties include spotting the ball (putting the ball down at the spot where play is to be resumed), whistling the play or the ball dead, pacing off the penalties, and acting as the final authority on the score.

**UMPIRE:** The umpire's main responsibility is the players' equipment and their conduct.

When play begins at the line of scrimmage, the umpire watches for illegal plays. He then moves downfield following the play action.

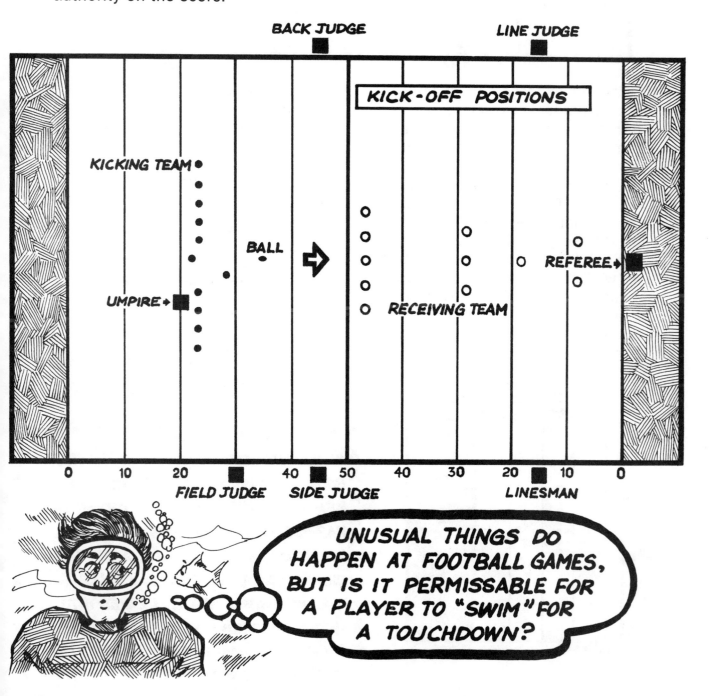

# AMERICAN FOOTBALL

## THE OFFICIALS

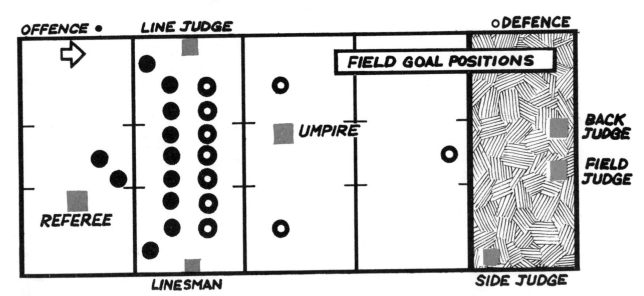

**LINESMAN:** The linesman's main responsibility is to watch for infractions at the neutral zone at the start of a down (off-side). He is in charge also of the yardage chains operated by two men on the sidelines. The yardage chains are the official 10 yard measurement used to see if a team has advanced the ball far enough for a first down. As well, the linesman must keep an accurate record of the down. There is a large "down indicator" sign on the sidelines that is under his control.

**FIELD JUDGE:** The field judge is really an extension of the referee, acting for the referee on downfield plays. If for any reason, the back judge must leave the game, the field judge takes over his responsibilities.

**BACK JUDGE:** The back judge is primarily concerned with maintaining an accurate time on the game as well as side line infractions.

**NOTE:** All officials can call all infractions, even in areas outside their primary responsibilities.

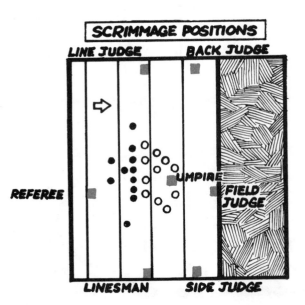

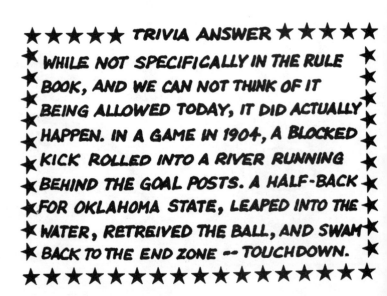

★★★★★ TRIVIA ANSWER ★★★★★
WHILE NOT SPECIFICALLY IN THE RULE
BOOK, AND WE CAN NOT THINK OF IT
BEING ALLOWED TODAY, IT DID ACTUALLY
HAPPEN. IN A GAME IN 1904, A BLOCKED
KICK ROLLED INTO A RIVER RUNNING
BEHIND THE GOAL POSTS. A HALF-BACK
FOR OKLAHOMA STATE, LEAPED INTO THE
WATER, RETREIVED THE BALL, AND SWAM
BACK TO THE END ZONE -- TOUCHDOWN.
★★★★★★★★★★★★★★★★★

## THE SNAP

One player, usually the center, passes the ball between his legs to a player behind him. The action must be smooth and continuous. The snapper may not slide his hands along the ball, lift his hands or move his feet until the snap is completed.

JOE NAMATH WAS TEMPORARILY SUSPENDED AT THE START OF THE 1969 SEASON. WHY?

THE CENTER HAS 3 DIFFERENT SNAPS HE MUST BE ABLE TO MAKE:

1. THE ONE PICTURED ABOVE IS USED ON MOST PLAYS.
2. ON SOME PASSING PLAYS, THE QUARTERBACK WILL STAND 5 OR 6 YARDS BACK FROM THE CENTER WHO MUST PASS IT SMOOTHLY BETWEEN HIS LEGS TO THE Q.B.
3. ON A PUNT, CONVERT, OR FIELD GOAL ATTEMPT, THE CENTER MUST ACCURATELY HEAVE THE BALL BETWEEN HIS LEGS BACK ABOUT 15 YARDS TO THE WAITING KICKER.

# AMERICAN FOOTBALL

## PENALTIES ON THE SNAP

**1. false start:** 5 yards

**2. player out-of-bounds on snap:** 5 yards

**3. more than 11 players on the field at the snap:** 5 yards

★★★★★★★★★★★★★★★★★★★★ *TRIVIA ANSWER* ★★★★★★★★★★★★★★★★★★★★
JOE WAS PART OWNER OF A BAR CALLED BATCHELORS III.
ALLEGEDLY IT WAS A BOOKMAKERS' MEETING PLACE.
JOE HAD TO SELL HIS SHARE OF THE BAR BEFORE HE
WAS REINSTATED INTO THE NFL.
★★★★★★★★★★★★★★★★★★★★★★★★★★★★★★★★★★★★★★★★★★★★

## PENALTIES ON THE SNAP

4. **offside or encroachment** : a player crossing the opponent's line of scrimmage before the ball is snapped: 5 yards

5. **man in motion** : an offensive backfield player moving incorrectly before the ball is snapped: 5 yards

# AMERICAN FOOTBALL

## DEFENSE

### What The Defense Does

The defense must stop the offense from getting the needed 10 yards for a first down and from scoring. They have two basic assignments — tackle the runner and break up plays.

To tackle a runner, the defenders try to pull, push, grab, or knock him to the ground. A runner is tackled if he is on the ground, in the hold of a defender and unable to move any further forward, or is under a group of defenders.

The defenders face many obstacles. The runner often has a good head of steam up and is hard to hold onto. The runner also lifts his knees high to discourage would-be tacklers.

And, of course, the runner knows what he's going to do (cut left or right, stop and spin) and the defender must wait and react. In addition to all that, there are the offensive blockers to contend with. Then, if all that is not enough, the offensive pass receivers will run their pass patterns on nearly every play so the safeties must follow them.

The defenders work to cover the offense while the offense tries to beat the defensive coverage.

### Defensive Positions

The defensive team basically has three positions; defensive linemen, linebackers, and defensive backs.

### Defensive Linemen

The defensive linemen take positions on the line of scrimmage facing the offensive linemen. Their jobs are to rush and if possible sack the quarterback and to stop any ball carrier trying to break through the line.

The defensive linemen almost always move forward when the ball is snapped. Prior to the snap, the defensive captain has called out the defensive formation to use.

The number of defensive linemen used on a play depends entirely on the defensive formation called (which depends on what offense the defensive captain is expecting).

The defensive linemen on the ends are often called defensive ends. The linemen between the ends are the defensive tackles. The middle defensive tackle is the nose guard — named the nose guard because he lines up nose-to-nose against the offensive center.

DEFENSIVE LINEMEN (4-3 SET)

ONE PLAYER IS DESIGNATED BY THE COACH, OFTEN THE DEFENSIVE CAPTAIN, TO ASSESS THE OFFENSIVE SITUATION. DEPENDING UPON SUCH ELEMENTS AS: THE DOWN, THE SCORE, THE TEAM, THE FIELD CONDITIONS, YARD LINE, HE CALLS THE DEFENSIVE FORMATION TO BE USED.

## DEFENSE

### Linebackers

The linebackers, as their name implies, line up directly behind the defensive linemen. Sometimes they line up right at the line of scrimmage slotting themselves between the tackles. When watching, you can tell the defensive tackles from the linebackers by their stance on the line. The linemen crouch for power. The line backers usually stand upright.

The linebackers defend against all plays — the passing and the rushing. And sometimes they will even rush the quarterback with the defensive linemen. Linebackers are further differentiated as outside linebackers (on the ends), inside linebackers and middle linebackers.

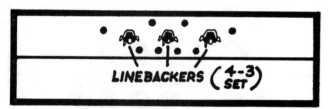

### Defensive Backs

The defensive backs are behind the linebackers and are called the secondary (sometimes the defensive backfield). Primarily, they are pass defenders, but if a ball carrier breaks through, the defensive backs are the last line of defense in front of the goal line. If a runner must be stopped by the secondary, he has made a good gain.

The defensive backs who are closest to the sidelines are called cornerbacks. Those in the middle are the safeties.

DEFENSIVE LINES GET STRANGE NICKNAMES. WHO, OR WHAT WERE THE "STEEL CURTAIN", "THE SACK EXCHANGE," AND THE "FEARSOME FOURSOME"?

## DEFENSIVE PLAYS

### Stack

A linebacker lines up directly behind a defensive lineman. This allows the linebackers to charge from any direction, right, left or straight ahead. The offensive line now must worry about where the defenders are going to come from.

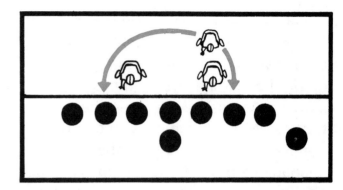

### Slants

When a slant is called, the defensive linemen all charge to the right or left instead of straight ahead. Since the defenders know what they intend to do, a slant call gives them a slight edge on the line.

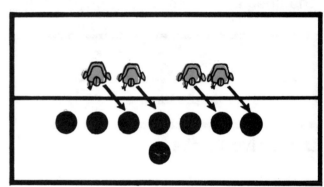

### Pinch

This is similar to a two-on-one block. The defensive linemen line up facing the spaces between the offensive linemen. The point of this play is to take a specific blocker completely out of the action.

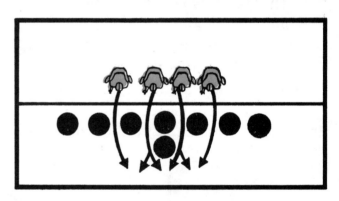

★★★★★★★★★★★★★ TRIVIA ANSWER ★★★★★★★★★★★★★★
ALL WERE DEFENSIVE LINEMEN - FEARSOME FOURSOME; LOS ANGELES RAMS:
DEACON JONES, CORY BACON, MERLIN OLSEN, BABA BROWN
SACK EXCHANGE; NEW YORK JETS:
MARK GASTINEAU, MARTY LYONS, ABDUL SALAARM, JOE KLECKO
STEEL CURTAIN; PITTSBURGH STEELERS:
"MEAN" JOE GREENE, DWIGHT WHITE, ERNIE HOLMES, L.C. GREENWOOD

## DEFENSE

### Stunts

A stunt is where the defenders exchange the paths they usually follow with each other. It can be between defensive linemen, linebackers, linemen with linebackers, etc. The point of a stunt is to confuse the offense and open up a direct hole to the quarterback.

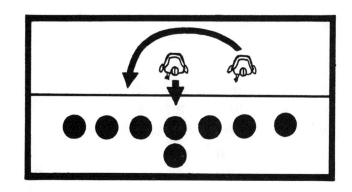

### The Blitz

This is a defensive play designed to sack the quarterback on what the defenders believe is a pass play. On a blitz, the secondary on their own or with the linebackers rush the passer. A blitz to be really successful must be a surprise. If the quarterback picks up that a blitz is coming, he'll call an audible on the line and probably set up a quick screen pass over the heads of the onrushing defenders.

In this game of deception and counter-deception, the defense will sometimes fake a blitz to force the quarterback into an audible. The hope here is that the change will cause confusion for the offense.

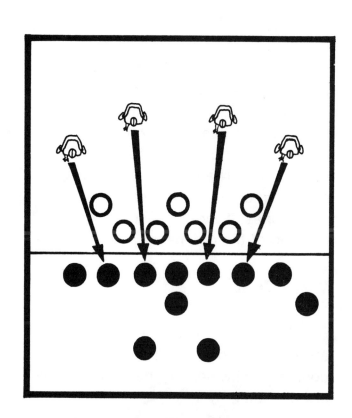

### Dogs

A dog is a type of blitz that can be used against both a run or a pass. Here a linebacker or linebackers roar into the offensive backfield right as the ball is snapped.

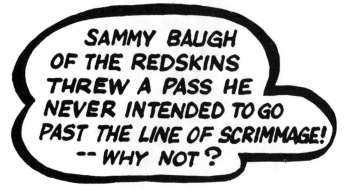

SAMMY BAUGH OF THE REDSKINS THREW A PASS HE NEVER INTENDED TO GO PAST THE LINE OF SCRIMMAGE! -- WHY NOT?

## PASS COVERAGE

### Zone Defenses

In this defense pattern, each pass defender is responsible for a specific area of the field — a zone. If an offensive receiver moves into the zone, that defender follows him, turning the receiver over to the next defender when the receiver changes zones.

### Strong Zone

The defended area of the field where a pass could be thrown is divided into four short pass zones and three long or deep pass zones. Three linebackers and a cornerback take the short zones. The two safeties and the other cornerback drop back into the deep zones. It looks like a clockwise rotation of the defense.

### Weak Zone

This is almost the opposite of the strong zone coverage. Here the shift is counterclockwise, but the assignments are the same.

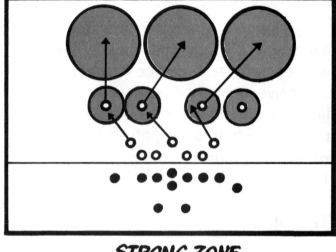

STRONG ZONE

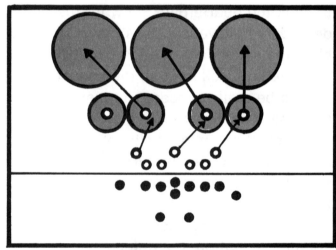

WEAK ZONE

IN A ZONE DEFENSE, THE PASS DEFENDERS DO NOT REACT TO THE RECEIVERS UNTIL THE BALL IS THROWN. AS SOON AS THE BALL IS IN THE AIR, ALL THE DEFENDERS MOVE TOWARD THE RECEIVER.

## DEFENSE

### Double Zones

The defended area of the field is divided into five short zones and two deep zones. Both cornerbacks and the three linebackers move into the short zones. The safeties cover the deep zones. This defends well against a short pass, but if a receiver gets into that gap between the deep zones, the defense is in big trouble.

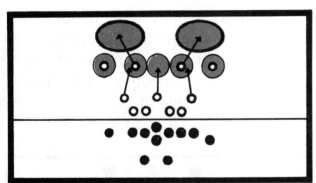

**DOUBLE ZONES**

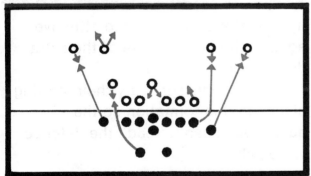

**MAN-TO-MAN COVERAGE**

### Bump and Run

A defensive back is allowed to hit an eligible receiver as he starts downfield within five yards of the line of scrimmage. To carry out a bump and run, the defensive back lines up directly in front of the receiver. When the receiver starts his move downfield, the defensive back moves into the receiver and bumps him. After that contact, the defender follows the eligible receiver downfield.

The point of the bump is to throw the timing of the passing play off — even if it's just a split second delay it could be enough to break up the pass play's success.

### Man-to-Man Coverage

This pass defense requires a lot from the defenders and is open to long passes being completed. Man-to-man coverage is not used very often.

In this defense, the linebackers cover the running backs, the cornerbacks cover the wide receivers, the strong safety covers the tight end, and the other safety, the free safety, moves anywhere, trying to be where the ball is going.

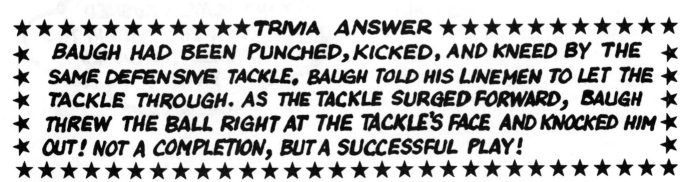

★ ★ ★ ★ ★ ★ ★ ★ ★ ★ ★ TRIVIA ANSWER ★ ★ ★ ★ ★ ★ ★ ★ ★ ★ ★
★ BAUGH HAD BEEN PUNCHED, KICKED, AND KNEED BY THE ★
★ SAME DEFENSIVE TACKLE. BAUGH TOLD HIS LINEMEN TO LET THE ★
★ TACKLE THROUGH. AS THE TACKLE SURGED FORWARD, BAUGH ★
★ THREW THE BALL RIGHT AT THE TACKLE'S FACE AND KNOCKED HIM ★
★ OUT! NOT A COMPLETION, BUT A SUCCESSFUL PLAY! ★
★ ★ ★ ★ ★ ★ ★ ★ ★ ★ ★ ★ ★ ★ ★ ★ ★ ★ ★ ★ ★ ★ ★ ★ ★ ★ ★ ★ ★

# AMERICAN FOOTBALL

## DEFENSE

## DEFENSIVE FORMATIONS

### 3-4 Defense

This defense calls for a three man defensive line — a nose tackle and two defensive ends. The nose tackle goes nose-to-nose with the offensive center. The ends are off slightly to the side of the offensive tackles.

Behind these defensive linemen (called down linesmen because they are the only defensive players to go into a crouch or 3 point stance) are four linebackers. Two outside linebackers are positioned outside the defensive ends. The inside linebackers move around the area between the two defensive ends.

In this defense pattern, the linebackers can rush the passer, stay in the secondary for defense against the break out run or move back to beef up the pass coverage.

The defensive ends must decide almost immediately after the snap whether the play is going to be a run or a pass. On a running play, they follow the flow and go after the ball carrier. On a pass, their job is to rush the passer and put pressure on him in the hope of making the passer rush the pass and maybe make a serious mistake.

### 4-3 Defense

When the offense must pass, the defense most likely will use the 4-3 defense.

In this formation, two defensive tackles set up directly in front of the offensive guards. Two defensive ends play outside the tackles and face the offensive tackles.

The middle linebacker stands between and behind the defensive tackles. One linebacker is over on the tight end's side. The other linebacker takes the other side of the line.

While this is a good defense

against the pass, it is also effective against the run because of the extra down lineman up front.

The linebackers vary their starting places in this formation so the quarterback can't "read" the defense too easily.

WHAT PLAYER RUSHED FOR OVER 200 YARDS IN TWO CONSECUTIVE GAMES –TWICE?

## DEFENSE

### The Flex

The flex is defined as a flexible 4-3 defense. This defense puts seven defenders near the line of scrimmage — four down linemen and three linebackers. Two down linemen set up in the regular stance on the line, ready to rush. The other two set up a few yards back of the line almost as linebackers but in a down stance.

In this defense, all but the two front down linemen hesitate after the snap — they don't rush in immediately. They try to read the play and then react to it.

This defense is fairly good against the run but is weak against the pass. It plugs up holes to stop the run but it gives the passer extra time to get his pass off.

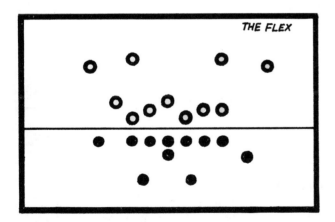

THE FLEX

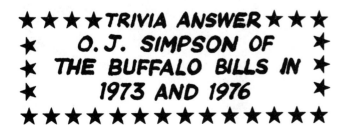

★★★★TRIVIA ANSWER★★★
★ O.J. SIMPSON OF ★
★ THE BUFFALO BILLS IN ★
★ 1973 AND 1976 ★
★★★★★★★★★★★★★★★★

### 6-5 or Goal Line Defense

When the ball is close, within a few yards of the goal line, a special defense is used. In the 6-5, there are six down linemen and five linebackers up front. Since there can't be a long pass, they don't have to defend against it. So the five linebackers defend against the short pass and the six down linemen are prepared for the short run.

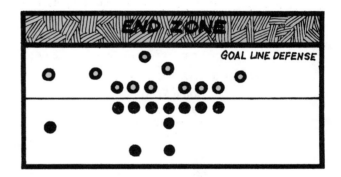

END ZONE

GOAL LINE DEFENSE

### The Nickel Defense

A nickel is five cents. The nickel defense uses five defensive backs. The extra back is called the nickel back. In this defense there are either three linebackers and three down linemen or two linebackers and four down linemen.

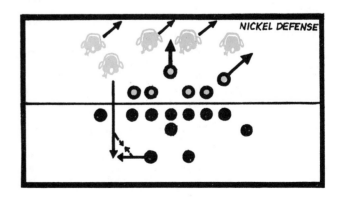

NICKEL DEFENSE

# AMERICAN FOOTBALL

## NATIONAL FOOTBALL CONFERENCE TEAMS

### Dallas Cowboys

**Home Field:** Texas Stadium
**Capacity:** 65,101
**Team Colors:** Royal Blue, Metallic Blue, and White

#### Individual Player's Records

| Action/Record | Player/Year |
|---|---|
| Most yards rushing in one game / 206 | Tony Dorsett / 1978 |
| Most yards rushing in one season / 1,646 | Tony Dorsett / 1981 |
| Most TD passes thrown in one game / 5 | Eddie Le Baron / 1962 |
| | Don Meredith / 1966 / 1968 |
| | Craig Morton / 1969 / 1970 |
| | Danny White / 1983 |
| Most TD passes thrown in one season / 29 | Danny White / 1983 |
| Most TD passes caught in one game / 4 | Bob Hayes / 1970 |
| Most TD passes caught in one season / 14 | Frank Clarke / 1962 |
| Most points scored in one game / 24 | Dan Reeves / 1967 |
| | Bob Hayes / 1970 |
| | Calvin Hill / 1971 |
| | Duane Thomas / 1971 |
| Most points scored in one season / 123 | Rafael Septien / 1983 |
| Most TD's scored in one game / 4 | Dan Reeves / 1967 |
| | Bob Hayes / 1970 |
| | Calvin Hill / 1971 |
| | Duane Thomas / 1971 |
| Most TD's scored in one season / 16 | Dan Reeves / 1966 |

### New York Giants

**Home Field:** Giants Stadium
**Capacity:** 76,891
**Team Colors:** Blue, Red, and White

#### Individual Player's Records

| Action/Record | Player/Year |
|---|---|
| Most yards rushing in one game / 218 | Gene Roberts / 1950 |
| Most yards rushing in one season / 1,182 | Ron Johnson / 1972 |
| Most TD passes thrown in one game / 7 | Y.A. Tittle / 1962 |
| Most TD passes thrown in one season / 36 | Y.A. Tittle / 1963 |
| Most TD passes caught in one game / 4 | Earnest Gray / 1980 |
| Most TD passes caught in one season / 13 | Homer Jones / 1967 |
| Most points scored in one game / 24 | Ron Johnson / 1972 |
| | Earnest Gray / 1980 |
| Most points scored in one season / 127 | Ali Haji-Sheikh / 1983 |
| Most TD's scored in one game / 4 | Ron Johnson / 1972 |
| | Earnest Gray / 1980 |
| Most TD's scored in one season / 17 | Gene Roberts / 1949 |

### Philadelphia Eagles

**Home Field:** Veterans Stadium
**Capacity:** 73,484
**Team Colors:** Kelly Green, White, and Silver

#### Individual Player's Records

| Action/Record | Player/Year |
|---|---|
| Most yards rushing in one game / 205 | Steve Van Buren / 1949 |
| Most yards rushing in one season / 1,512 | Wilbert Montgomery / 1979 |
| Most TD passes thrown in one game / 7 | Adrian Burk / 1954 |
| Most TD passes thrown in one season / 32 | Sonny Jurgenson / 1961 |
| Most TD passes caught in one game / 4 | Joe Carter / 1934 |
| | Ben Hawkins / 1969 |
| Most TD passes caught in one season / 13 | Tommy McDonald / 1960 / 1961 |
| | Mike Quick / 1983 |
| Most points scored in one game / 25 | Bobby Walston / 1954 |
| Most points scored in one season / 116 | Paul McFadden / 1984 |

| Most TD's scored in one game / 4 | Joe Carter / 1934 |
| | Clarence Peaks / 1958 |
| | Tommy McDonald / 1959 |
| | Ben Hawkins / 1969 |
| | Wilbert Montgomery / 1978 / 1979 |
| Most TD's scored in one season / 18 | Steve Van Buren / 1945 |

## St. Louis Cardinals

**Home Field:** Busch Stadium
**Capacity:** 51,392
**Team Colors:** Cardinal Red, White, and Black

### Individual Player's Records

| Action/Record | Player/Year |
| --- | --- |
| Most yards rushing in one game / 203 | John Crow / 1960 |
| Most yards rushing in one season / 1,605 | Ottis Anderson / 1979 |
| Most TD passes thrown in one game / 6 | Jim Hardy / 1950 |
| | Charley Johnson / 1965 / 1969 |
| Most TD passes thrown in one season / 28 | Charley Johnson / 1963 |
| | Neil Lomax / 1984 |
| Most TD passes caught in one game / 5 | Bob Shaw / 1950 |
| Most TD passes caught in one season / 15 | Sonny Randle / 1960 |
| Most points scored in one game / 40 | Ernie Nevers / 1929 |
| Most points scored in one season / 117 | Jim Bakken / 1967 |
| | Neil O'Donoghue / 1984 |
| Most TD's scored in one game / 6 | Ernie Nevers / 1929 |
| Most TD's scored in one season / 17 | John Crow / 1962 |

## Washington Redskins

**Home Field:** Robert F. Kennedy Stadium
**Capacity:** 55,431
**Team Colors:** Burgundy and Gold

### Individual Player's Records

| Action/Record | Player/Year |
| --- | --- |
| Most yards rushing in one game / 195 | Mike Thomas / 1976 |
| Most yards rushing in one season / 1,347 | John Riggins / 1983 |
| Most TD passes thrown in one game / 6 | Sam Baugh / 1943 / 1947 |
| Most TD passes thrown in one season / 31 | Sonny Jurgenson / 1967 |
| Most TD passes caught in one game / 3 | Hugh Taylor / 1952 |
| | Jerry Smith / 1967 / 1969 |
| | Pat Richter / 1968 |
| | Larry Brown / 1973 |
| | Jean Fugett / 1976 |
| | Albin Garrett / 1982 |
| | Art Monk / 1984 |
| Most TD passes caught in one season / 12 | Hugh Taylor / 1952 |
| | Charley Taylor / 1966 |
| | Jerry Smith / 1967 |
| Most points scored in one game / 24 | Dick James / 1961 |
| | Larry Brown / 1973 |
| Most points scored in one season / 161 | Mark Moseley / 1983 |
| Most TD's scored in one game / 4 | Dick James / 1961 |
| | Larry Brown / 1973 |
| Most TD's scored in one season / 24 | John Riggins / 1983 |

## Chicago Bears

**Home Field:** Soldier Field
**Capacity:** 65,793
**Team Colors:** Orange, Navy Blue, and White

### Individual Player's Records

| Action/Record | Player/Year |
| --- | --- |
| Most yards rushing in one game / 275 | Walter Payton / 1977 |

| Most yards rushing in one season / 1,852 | Walter Payton / 1977 |
| Most TD passes thrown in one game / 7 | Sid Luckman / 1943 |
| Most TD passes caught in one game / 4 | Harlon Hill / 1954 |
| | Mike Ditka / 1963 |
| Most TD passes caught in one season / 13 | Dick Gordon / 1970 |
| | Ken Kananaugh / 1947 |
| Most points scored in one game / 36 | Gale Sayers / 1965 |
| Most points scored in one season / 132 | Gale Sayers / 1965 |
| Most TD's scored in one game / 3 | Gale Sayers / 1965 |
| Most TD's scored in one season / 22 | Gale Sayers / 1965 |

## Detroit Lions

**Home Field:** Pontiac Silverdome
**Capacity:** 80,638
**Team Colors:** Honolulu Blue and Silver

### Individual Player's Records

| Action/Record | Player/Year |
|---|---|
| Most yards rushing in one game / 198 | Bob Hoernschermeyer / 1950 |
| Most yards rushing in one season / 1,437 | Billy Sims / 1981 |
| Most TD passes thrown in one game / 5 | Gary Danielson / 1978 |
| Most TD passes thrown in one season / 26 | Bobby Layne / 1951 |
| Most TD passes caught in one game / 4 | Cloyce Box / 1950 |
| Most TD passes caught in one season / 15 | Cloyce Box / 1952 |
| Most points scored in one game / 24 | Cloyce Box / 1950 |
| Most points scored in one season / 128 | Doak Walker / 1950 |
| Most TD's scored in one game / 4 | Cloyce Box / 1950 |
| Most TD's scored in one season / 16 | Billy Sims / 1980 |

## Green Bay Packers

**Home Field:** County Stadium, Milwaukee
**Capacity:** 55,958
**Team Colors:** Green and Gold

### Individual Player's Records

| Action/Record | Player/Year |
|---|---|
| Most yards rushing in one game / 186 | Jim Taylor / 1961 |
| Most yards rushing in one season / 1,474 | Jim Taylor / 1962 |
| Most TD passes thrown in one game / 5 | Cecil Osbell / 1942 |
| | Don Horn / 1969 |
| | Lynn Dickey / 1981 / 1983 |
| Most TD passes thrown in one season / 32 | Lynn Dickey / 1983 |
| Most TD passes caught in one game / 4 | Don Hutson / 1945 |
| Most TD passes caught in one season / 17 | Don Hutson / 1943 |
| Most points scored in one game / 33 | Paul Horning / 1961 |
| Most points scored in one season / 176 | Paul Hornung / 1960 |
| Most TD's scored in one game / 5 | Paul Hornung / 1961 |
| Most TD's scored in one season / 19 | Jim Taylor / 1962 |

## Minnesota Vikings

**Home Field:** Hubert H. Humphrey Metrodome
**Capacity:** 62,212
**Team Colors:** Purple, White, and Gold

### Individual Player's Records

| Action/Record | Player/Year |
|---|---|
| Most yards rushing in one game / 200 | Chuck Foreman / 1976 |
| Most yards rushing in one season / 1,155 | Chuck Foreman / 1976 |
| Most TD passes thrown in one game / 7 | Joe Kapp / 1969 |
| Most TD passes thrown in one season / 26 | Tommy Kramer / 1981 |
| Most TD passes caught in one game / 4 | Ahmad Rashad / 1979 |
| Most TD passes caught in one season / 11 | Jerry Reichow / 1961 |

# AMERICAN FOOTBALL

| Most points scored in one game / 24 | Chuck Foreman / 1975 |
| | Ahmad Rashad / 1979 |
| Most points scored in one season / 132 | Chuck Foreman / 1975 |
| Most TD's scored in one game / 4 | Chuck Foreman / 1975 |
| | Ahmad Rashad / 1979 |
| Most TD's scored in one season / 22 | Chuck Foreman / 1975 |

## Tampa Bay Buccaneers

**Home Field:** Tampa Stadium
**Capacity:** 74,317
**Team Colors:** Florida Orange, White, and Red

### Individual Player's Records

| Action/Record | Player/Year |
|---|---|
| Most yards rushing in one game / 219 | James Wilder / 1983 |
| Most yards rushing in one season / 1,544 | James Wilder / 1984 |
| Most TD passes thrown in one game / 4 | Doug Williams / 1980 / 1981 |
| | Jack Thompson / 1983 |
| Most TD passes thrown in one season / 20 | Doug Williams / 1980 |
| Most TD passes caught in one game / 3 | Morris Owens / 1976 |
| Most TD passes caught in one season / 9 | Kevin House / 1981 |
| Most points scored in one game / 18 | Morris Owens / 1976 |
| Most points scored in one season / 95 | Obed Ariri / 1984 |
| Most TD's scored in one game / 3 | Morris Owens / 1976 |
| Most TD's scored in one season / 13 | James Wilder / 1984 |

## Atlanta Falcons

**Home Field:** Atlanta Stadium
**Capacity:** 60,748
**Team Colors:** Red, Black, Silver, and White

### Individual Player's Records

| Action/Record | Player/Year |
|---|---|
| Most yards rushing in one game / 167 | William Andrews / 1979 |
| Most yards rushing in one season / 1,567 | William Andrews / 1983 |
| Most TD passes thrown in one game / 4 | Randy Johnson / 1969 |
| | Steve Bartkowski / 1980 / 1981 |
| Most TD passes thrown in one season / 31 | Steve Bartkowski / 1980 |
| Most TD passes caught in one game / 3 | Alfred Jenkins / 1981 |
| Most TD passes caught in one season / 13 | Alfred Jenkins / 1981 |
| Most points scored in one game / 18 | Lynn Cain / 1979 |
| | Alfred Jenkins / 1981 |
| | William Andrews / 1982 / 1983 |
| Most points scored in one season / 114 | Mike Ruckhurst / 1981 |
| Most TD's scored in one game / 3 | Lynn Caine / 1979 |
| | Alfred Jenkins / 1981 |
| | William Andrews / 1982 / 1983 |
| Most TD's scored in one season / 13 | Alfred Jenkins / 1981 |

## Los Angeles Rams

**Home Field:** Anaheim Stadium
**Capacity:** 69,007
**Team Colors:** Royal Blue, Gold, and White

### Individual Player's Records

| Action/Record | Player/Year |
|---|---|
| Most yards rushing in one game / 247 | Willie Ellison / 1971 |
| Most yards rushing in one season / 2,105 | Eric Dickerson / 1984 |
| Most TD passes thrown in one game / 5 | Bob Waterfield / 1949 |
| | Norm Van Brocklin / 1950 / 1951 |
| | Roman Gabriel / 1965 |
| | Vince Ferragamo / 1980 / 1983 |
| Most TD passes thrown in one season / 30 | Vince Ferragamo / 1980 |

| | |
|---|---|
| Most TD passes caught in one game / 4 | Bob Shaw / 1949 |
| | Elroy Hirsch / 1951 |
| | Harold Jackson / 1973 |
| Most TD passes caught in one season / 17 | Elroy Hirsch / 1951 |
| Most points scored in one game / 24 | Elroy Hirsch / 1951 |
| | Bob Shaw / 1949 |
| | Harold Jackson / 1973 |
| Most points scored in one season / 130 | David Roy / 1973 |
| Most TD's scored in one game / 4 | Elroy Hirsch / 1951 |
| | Bob Shaw / 1949 |
| | Harold Jackson / 1973 |
| Most TD's scored in one season / 20 | Eric Dickerson / 1983 |

## New Orleans Saints

**Home Field:** Superdome
**Capacity:** 71,684
**Team Colors:** Gold, Black, and White

### Individual Player's Records

| Action/Record | Player/Year |
|---|---|
| Most yards rushing in one game / 206 | George Rogers / 1983 |
| Most yards rushing in one season / 1,674 | George Rogers / 1981 |
| Most TD passes thrown in one game / 6 | Billy Kilmer / 1969 |
| Most TD passes thrown in one season / 23 | Archie Manning / 1980 |
| Most TD passes caught in one game / 3 | Dan Abramowicz / 1971 |
| Most TD passes caught in one season / 9 | Henry Childs / 1977 |
| Most points scored in one game / 18 | Walt Roberts / 1967 |
| | Dan Abramowicz / 1971 |
| | Archie Manning / 1977 |
| | Chuck Muncie / 1979 |
| | George Rogers / 1981 |
| | Wayne Wilson / 1982 |
| Most points scored in one season / 99 | Tom Dempsey / 1969 |
| Most TD's scored in one game / 3 | Walt Roberts / 1967 |
| | Dan Abramowicz / 1971 |
| | Archie Manning / 1977 |
| | Chuck Muncie / 1979 |
| | George Rogers / 1981 |
| | Wayne Wilson / 1982 |
| Most TD's scored in one season / 13 | George Rogers / 1981 |

## San Francisco 49ers

**Home Field:** Candlestick Park
**Capacity:** 61,185
**Team Colors:** Gold and Scarlet

### Individual Player's Records

| Action/Record | Player/Year |
|---|---|
| Most yards rushing in one game / 194 | Delvin Williams / 1976 |
| Most yards rushing in one season / 1,203 | Delvin Williams / 1976 |
| Most TD passes thrown in one game / 5 | Frank Albert / 1949 |
| | John Brodie / 1965 |
| | Steve Spurvier / 1972 |
| Most TD passes thrown in one season / 30 | John Brodie / 1965 |
| Most TD passes caught in one game / 3 | Alyn Beals / 1948 / 1949 |
| | Gordy Soltau / 1951 |
| | Bernie Casey / 1962 |
| | Dave Parks / 1965 |
| | Gene Washington / 1972 |
| Most TD passes caught in one season / 14 | Alyn Beals / 1948 |
| Most points scored in one game / 26 | Gordy Soltau / 1951 |
| Most points scored in one season / 131 | Ray Wersching / 1984 |
| Most TD's scored in one game / 4 | Bill Kilmer / 1961 |
| Most TD's scored in one season / 14 | Alyn Beals / 1948 |

# AMERICAN FOOTBALL

## AMERICAN FOOTBALL CONFERENCE TEAMS

### Buffalo Bills

**Home Field:** Rich Stadium
**Capacity:** 80,290
**Team Colors:** Scarlet, Royal Blue, and White

#### Individual Player's Records

| Action/Record | Player/Year |
|---|---|
| Most yards rushing in one game / 173 | O.J. Simpson / 1976 |
| Most yards rushing in one season / 2,003 | O.J. Simpson / 1973 |
| Most TD passes thrown in one game / 5 | Joe Ferguson / 1979 |
| Most TD passes thrown in one season / 26 | Joe Ferguson / 1983 |
| Most TD passes caught in one game / 4 | Jerry Butler / 1979 |
| Most TD passes caught in one season / 10 | Elbert Dubenion / 1964 |
| Most points scored in one game / 30 | Cookie Gilchrist / 1963 |
| Most points scored in one season / 138 | O.J. Simpson / 1975 |
| Most TD's scored in one game / 5 | Cookie Gilchrist / 1963 |
| Most TD's scored in one season / 23 | O.J. Simpson / 1975 |

### Indianapolis Colts

**Home Field:** Hoosier Dome
**Capacity:** 60,127
**Team Colors:** Royal Blue and White

#### Individual Player's Records

| Action/Record | Player/Year |
|---|---|
| Most yards rushing in one game / 198 | Norm Bulaich / 1971 |
| Most yards rushing in one season / 1,200 | Lydell Mitchell / 1976 |
| Most TD passes thrown in one game / 5 | Gary Cuozzo / 1965 |
| Most TD passes thrown in one season / 32 | John Unitas / 1959 |
| Most TD passes caught in one game / 3 | Jim Mutscheller / 1957 |
| | Raymond Berry / 1960 |
| | Jimmy Orr / 1962 / 1964 |
| | Roger Carr / 1976 |
| Most TD passes caught in one season / 14 | Raymond Berry / 1959 |
| Most points scored in one game / 24 | Lenny Moore / 1958 / 1960 / 1961 |
| | Lydell Mitchell / 1975 |
| Most points scored in one season / 120 | Lenny Moore / 1964 |
| Most TD's scored in one game / 4 | Lenny Moore / 1958 / 1960 / 1961 |
| | Lydell Mitchell / 1975 |
| Most TD's scored in one season / 20 | Lenny Moore / 1964 |

### Miami Dolphins

**Home Field:** Orange Bowl
**Capacity:** 75,206
**Team Colors:** Aqua and Orange

#### Individual Player's Records

| Action/Record | Player/Year |
|---|---|
| Most yards rushing in one game / 197 | Mercury Morris / 1973 |
| Most yards rushing in one season / 1,258 | Delvin Williams / 1978 |
| Most TD passes thrown in one game / 6 | Bob Grieve / 1977 |
| Most TD passes thrown in one season / 48 | Dan Marino / 1984 |
| Most TD passes caught in one game / 4 | Paul Warfield / 1973 |
| Most TD passes caught in one season / 18 | Mark Clayton / 1984 |
| Most points scored in one game / 24 | Paul Warfield / 1973 |
| Most points scored in one season / 117 | Garo Yepremian / 1971 |
| Most TD's scored in one game / 4 | Paul Warfield / 1973 |
| Most TD's scored in one season / 18 | Mark Clayton / 1984 |

### New England Patriots

**Home Field:** Sullivan Stadium
**Capacity:** 60,890
**Team Colors:** Red, White, and Blue

# AMERICAN FOOTBALL

## Individual Player's Records

| Action/Record | Player/Year |
|---|---|
| Most yards rushing in one game / 212 | Tony Collins / 1983 |
| Most yards rushing in one season / 1,458 | Jim Nance / 1966 |
| Most TD passes thrown in one game / 5 | Babe Parilli / 1964 / 1967 |
| | Steve Grogan / 1979 |
| Most TD passes thrown in one season / 31 | Babe Parilli / 1964 |
| Most TD passes caught in one game / 3 | Billy Lott / 1961 |
| | Gino Cappelletti / 1964 |
| | Jim Whalen / 1967 |
| | Harold Jackson / 1979 |
| | Derrick Ramsey / 1984 |
| Most TD passes caught in one season / 12 | Stanley Morgan / 1979 |
| Most points scored in one game / 28 | Gino Cappelletti / 1965 |
| Most points scored in one season / 155 | Gino Cappelletti / 1964 |
| Most TD's scored in one game / 3 | Billy Lott / 1961 |
| | Larry Garron / 1964 / 1966 |
| | Gino Cappelletti / 1964 |
| | Jim Whalen / 1967 |
| | Sam Cunningham / 1974 / 1975 |
| | Mack Herron / 1974 |
| | Harold Jackson / 1979 |
| | Derrick Ramsey / 1984 |
| Most TD's scored in one season / 13 | Steve Grogan / 1976 |
| | Stanley Morgan / 1979 |

## New York Jets

**Home Field:** Giants Stadium
**Capacity:** 76,891
**Team Colors:** Kelly Green, and White

### Individual Player's Records

| Action/Record | Player/Year |
|---|---|
| Most yards rushing in one game / 180 | Matt Snell / 1964 |
| Most yards rushing in one season / 1,070 | Freeman McNeil / 1984 |
| Most TD passes thrown in one game / 6 | Joe Namath / 1972 |
| Most TD passes thrown in one season / 26 | Al Dorrow / 1960 |
| | Joe Namath / 1967 |
| Most TD passes caught in one game / 3 | Art Powell / 1960 |
| | Don Maynard / 1963 / 1967 / 1968 |
| | Rick Caster / 1972 |
| | Wesley Walker / 1982 / 1984 |
| Most TD passes caught in one season / 14 | Art Powell / 1960 |
| | Don Maynard / 1965 |
| Most points scored in one game / 19 | Jim Turner / 1968 |
| | Pat Leahy / 1984 |
| Most points scored in one season / 145 | Jim Turner / 1968 |
| Most TD's scored in one game / 3 | Art Powell / 1960 |
| | Don Maynard / 1963 / 1967 / 1968 |
| | Emerson Boozer / 1967 / 1972 |
| | Billy Joe / 1968 |
| | Rick Caster / 1972 |
| | John Riggins / 1974 |
| | Kevin Long / 1978 / 1979 |
| | Wesley Walker / 1982 / 1984 |
| Most TD's scored in one season / 14 | Art Powell / 1960 |
| | Don Maynard / 1965 |
| | Emerson Boozer / 1972 |

## Cincinnati Bengals

**Home Field:** Riverfront Stadium
**Capacity:** 59,754
**Team Colors:** Orange, Black, and White

# AMERICAN FOOTBALL

79

## Individual Player's Records

| Action/Record | Player/Year |
|---|---|
| Most yards rushing in one game / 160 | Pete Johnson / 1978 |
| Most yards rushing in one season / 1,077 | Pete Johnson / 1981 |
| Most TD passes thrown in one game / 4 | Greg Cook / 1969 |
| | Ken Anderson / 1976 |
| Most TD passes thrown in one season / 29 | Ken Anderson / 1981 |
| Most TD passes caught in one game / 3 | Bob Trumpy / 1969 |
| | Isaac Curtis / 1973 / 1979 |
| Most TD passes caught in one season / 10 | Isaac Curtis / 1974 |
| Most points scored in one game / 19 | Horst Muhlmann / 1970 / 1972 |
| Most points scored in one season / 115 | Jim Breech / 1981 |
| Most TD's scored in one game / 4 | Larry Kinnebreau / 1984 |
| Most TD's scored in one season / 16 | Pete Johnson / 1981 |

## Cleveland Browns

**Home Field:** Cleveland Stadium
**Capacity:** 80,098
**Team Colors:** Cleveland Brown, Orange, and White

### Individual Player's Records

| Action/Record | Player/Year |
|---|---|
| Most yards rushing in one game / 237 | Jim Brown / 1957 / 1961 |
| Most yards rushing in one season / 1,863 | Jim Brown / 1963 |
| Most TD passes thrown in one game / 5 | Frank Ryan / 1964 |
| | Bill Nelsen / 1969 |
| | Brian Sipe / 1979 |
| Most TD passes thrown in one season / 30 | Brian Sipe / 1980 |
| Most TD passes caught in one game / 3 | Mac Speedie / 1951 |
| | Darrell Brewster / 1953 |
| | Ray Renfro / 1959 |
| | Gary Collins / 1963 |
| | Reggie Rucker / 1976 |
| | Larry Poole / 1977 |
| | Calvin Hill / 1978 |
| Most TD passes caught in one season / 13 | Gary Collins / 1963 |
| Most points scored in one game / 36 | Dub Jones / 1951 |
| Most points scored in one season / 126 | Jim Brown / 1965 |
| Most TD's scored in one game / 6 | Dub Jones / 1951 |
| Most TD's scored in one season / 21 | Jim Brown / 1965 |

## Houston Oilers

**Home Field:** Astrodome
**Capacity:** 50,452
**Team Colors:** Scarlet, Blue, and White

### Individual Player's Records

| Action/Record | Player/Year |
|---|---|
| Most yards rushing in one game / 216 | Billy Cannon / 1961 |
| Most yards rushing in one season / 1,934 | Earl Campbell / 1980 |
| Most TD passes thrown in one game / 7 | George Blanda / 1961 |
| Most TD passes thrown in one season / 36 | George Blanda / 1961 |
| Most TD passes caught in one game / 3 | Bill Groman / 1960 / 1961 |
| | Billy Cannon / 1961 |
| | Charlie Hennigan / 1961 / 1963 |
| | Charles Frazier / 1966 |
| | Dave Casper / 1981 |
| Most TD passes caught in one season / 17 | Bill Groman / 1961 |
| Most points scored in one game / 30 | Billy Cannon / 1961 |
| Most points scored in one season / 115 | George Blanda / 1960 |
| Most TD's scored in one game / 5 | Billy Cannon / 1961 |
| Most TD's scored in one season / 19 | Earl Campbell / 1979 |

## Pittsburgh Steelers

**Home Field:** Three Rivers Stadium
**Capacity:** 59,000
**Team Colors:** Black and Gold

### Individual Player's Records

| Action/Record | Player/Year |
|---|---|
| Most yards rushing in one game / 218 | John Fuqua / 1970 |
| Most yards rushing in one season / 1,246 | Franco Harris / 1975 |
| Most TD passes thrown in one game / 5 | Terry Bradshaw / 1981 |
| Most TD passes thrown in one season / 28 | Terry Bradshaw / 1978 |
| Most TD passes caught in one game / 4 | Roy Jefferson / 1968 |
| Most TD passes caught in one season / 12 | Buddy Dial / 1961 |
| Most points scored in one game / 24 | Ray Mathews / 1954 |
| | Roy Jefferson / 1968 |
| Most points scored in one season / 123 | Roy Gerela / 1973 |
| Most TD's scored in one game / 4 | Ray Mathews / 1954 |
| | Roy Jefferson / 1968 |
| Most TD's scored in one season / 14 | Franco Harris / 1976 |

## Denver Broncos

**Home Field:** Mile High Stadium
**Capacity:** 75,100
**Team Colors:** Orange, Blue, and White

### Individual Player's Records

| Action/Record | Player/Year |
|---|---|
| Most yards rushing in one game / 183 | Otis Armstrong / 1974 |
| Most yards rushing in one season / 1,407 | Otis Armstrong / 1974 |
| Most TD passes thrown in one game / 5 | Frank Tripucka / 1962 |
| | John Elway / 1984 |
| Most TD passes thrown in one season / 24 | Frank Tripucka / 1960 |
| Most TD passes caught in one game / 3 | Lionel Taylor / 1960 |
| | Bob Scarpitto / 1966 |
| | Haven Moses / 1973 |
| | Steve Watson / 1981 |
| Most TD passes caught in one season / 13 | Steve Watson / 1981 |
| Most points scored in one game / 21 | Gene Mingo / 1960 |
| Most points scored in one season / 137 | Gene Mingo / 1962 |
| Most TD's scored in one game / 3 | Lionel Taylor / 1980 |
| | Jon Keyworth / 1974 |
| | Don Stone / 1962 |
| | Steve Watson / 1981 |
| | Bob Scarpitto / 1966 |
| | Floyd Little / 1972 / 1973 |
| | Haven Moses / 1973 |
| | Otis Armstrong / 1974 |
| Most TD's scored in one season / 13 | Floyd Little / 1972 / 1973 |
| | Steve Watson / 1981 |

## Kansas City Chiefs

**Home Field:** Arrowhead Stadium
**Capacity:** 78,094
**Team Colors:** Red and Gold

### Individual Player's Records

| Action/Record | Player/Year |
|---|---|
| Most yards rushing in one game / 193 | Joe Delaney / 1981 |
| Most yards rushing in one season / 1,121 | Joe Delaney / 1981 |
| Most TD passes thrown in one game / 6 | Len Dawson / 1964 |
| Most TD passes thrown in one season / 30 | Len Dawson / 1964 |
| Most TD passes caught in one game / 4 | Frank Jackson / 1964 |
| Most TD passes caught in one season / 12 | Chris Burford / 1962 |
| Most points scored in one game / 30 | Abner Haynes / 1961 |
| Most points scored in one season / 129 | Jan Stenerud / 1968 |

Most TD's scored in one game / 5 — Abner Haynes / 1961
Most TD's scored in one season / 19 — Abner Haynes / 1962

## Los Angeles Raiders

**Home Field:** Los Angeles Memorial Coliseum
**Capacity:** 92,600
**Team Colors:** Silver and Black

### Individual Player's Records

| Action/Record | Player/Year |
|---|---|
| Most yards rushing in one game / 200 | Clem Daniels / 1963 |
| Most yards rushing in one season / 1,273 | Mark van Eeghen / 1977 |
| Most TD passes thrown in one game / 6 | Tom Flores / 1963 |
|  | Daryle Lamonica / 1969 |
| Most TD passes thrown in one season / 34 | Daryle Lamonica / 1969 |
| Most TD passes caught in one game / 4 | Art Powell / 1963 |
| Most TD passes caught in one season / 16 | Art Powell / 1963 |
| Most points scored in one game / 24 | Art Powell / 1963 |
|  | Marcus Allen / 1984 |
| Most points scored in one season / 117 | George Blanda / 1968 |
| Most TD's scored in one game / 4 | Art Powell / 1963 |
|  | Marcus Allen / 1984 |
| Most TD's scored in one season / 18 | Marcus Allen / 1984 |

## San Diego Chargers

**Home Field:** San Diego Jack Murphy Stadium
**Capacity:** 60,100
**Team Colors:** Blue, Gold, and White

### Individual Player's Records

| Action/Record | Player/Year |
|---|---|
| Most yards rushing in one game / 206 | Keith Lincoln / 1964 |
| Most yards rushing in one season / 1,162 | Don Woods / 1974 |
| Most TD passes thrown in one game / 6 | Dan Fouts / 1981 |
| Most TD passes thrown in one season / 33 | Dan Fouts / 1981 |
| Most TD passes caught in one game / 5 | Kellen Winslow / 1981 |
| Most TD passes caught in one season / 14 | Lance Alworth / 1965 |
| Most points scored in one game / 30 | Kellen Winslow / 1981 |
| Most points scored in one season / 118 | Rolf Benirschke / 1980 |
| Most TD's scored in one game / 5 | Kellen Winslow / 1981 |
| Most TD's scored in one season / 19 | Chuck Muncie / 1981 |

## Seattle Seahawks

**Home Field:** Kingdome
**Capacity:** 64,757
**Team Colors:** Blue, Green, and Silver

### Individual Player's Records

| Action/Record | Player/Year |
|---|---|
| Most yards rushing in one game / 207 | Curt Warner / 1983 |
| Most yards rushing in one season / 1,449 | Curt Warner / 1983 |
| Most TD passes thrown in one game / 5 | Dane King / 1984 |
| Most TD passes thrown in one season / 22 | Jim Zorn / 190 |
| Most TD passes caught in one game / 3 | Steve Largent / 1983 / 1984 |
| Most TD passes caught in one season / 12 | Steve Largent / 1984 |
| Most points scored in one game / 18 | David Sims / 1978 |
|  | Sherman Smith / 1979 |
|  | Steve Largent / 1983 / 1984 |
|  | Curt Warnes / 1983 |
| Most points scored in one season / 110 | Norm Johnson / 1984 |
| Most TD's scored in one game / 4 | David Sims / 1978 |
|  | Sherman Smith / 1979 |
|  | Steve Largent / 1983 |
|  | Curt Warner / 1983 |
| Most TD's scored in one season / 15 | David Sims / 1978 |

## UNUSUAL FOOTBALL TERMS

**Animal:** a very wild player: usually a defensive lineman; doesn't always follow the "sportsmanlike" rules.

**Audible:** after the huddle the offense moves to the line; the quarterback sees something in the defense to make him want to change the play that was called; he shouts out a series of code words, phrases, or numbers to inform his team of the change; what he shouts out is called *an audible.*

**Bomb:** a long, floating pass.

**A BOMB**

**Bootleg:** a running play in which the quarterback carries the ball; often he fakes a handoff first.

**Broken-field running:** the ball carrier running through the different opponents trying to tackle him.

**Bullet:** a hard, straight, accurate forward pass; the quarterback is often said to *rifle the pass.*

**A BULLET**

**Buttonhook:** a pass pattern; the receiver runs downfield about 15 to 20 yards then abruptly reverses and runs back toward the quarterback — like a U-turn.

**Cadence:** the rhythm a quarterback uses in calling out the signals on the line; a quarterback may change his cadence to fool the defense and make them go offside.

**Clothesline tackle:** stopping the runner by extending your arm straight out and letting the runner's adam's apple hit it.

**CLOTHESLINE TACKLE**

**Coffin corner:** the corners of your end of the field near your end zone; that is the target of most punts.

**Counter play:** the quarterback and his blockers move one way while the ball is handed off to a runner going in the opposite direction.

**Cut:** change direction very suddenly.

EAT THE BALL

**Eat the ball:** when the quarterback knows he's about to be sacked and he has nowhere safe to throw the ball, he just accepts his fate and holds onto the ball *(eats the ball)* for a loss.

**Flanker:** referred to today as a wide receiver; a back moved away to the side of the line and about to run downfield for a pass.

**Flat:** this is the part of the field directly to the left or right of the line as seen by the quarterback.

**Gamer:** a player willing to play no matter what has happened to him or how he feels and does his best for as long as he can.

**Go against the grain:** move against the flow of the action.

**Grind it out:** make gains on the ground slowly but continuously.

**Hang time:** the length of time a kicked ball remains in the air: the longer the hang time the better as long as you still get good distance on the kick.

**Hitch:** a pass pattern; like a short buttonhook.

**In the trenches:** the action on the line.

ACTION IN THE TRENCHES

**Muff:** to botch up a play; usually used when a player recovers a fumbled ball only to fumble it again.

**Pit:** the trenches; the action on the line.

**Playbook:** the book (kept as secret as possible) in which a team keeps all its plays and their descriptions.

**Red dog:** this is a play in which the linebacker(s) go straight at the quarterback; it is a play with a message for the quarterback that the linebackers try to deliver personally.

**Rollout:** this is a quarterback's move; if he moves out of the pocket and down the line to throw or run, he *rolls out.*

**Sack:** to tackle the quarterback for a loss.

**Safety valve:** this player is the one the quarterback can quick dump a pass to if the quarterback sees he's in trouble with his primary receivers downfield.

**Scramble:** run any way you can to escape a tackle; usually this term is used for the quarterback after his pocket breaks down.

**Shank:** kick the ball off the side of your foot by mistake.

**Slot:** a position; it is one yard behind the line and a few yards off tackle but inside the wide receiver.

**Spike:** slam the ball straight down onto the ground; players who have just scored a touchdown often spike the ball in the end zone.

**SPIKING THE BALL**

**Squareout:** a pass pattern; the receiver runs straight downfield about 15 yards and then veers toward the sideline.

**Strip the ball:** tackle the ball player and the ball forcing the carrier to fumble.

**Throw the ball away:** if a quarterback sees all his receivers are very closely covered by opponents, he may throw the ball into a safe area of the field where it won't be caught or intercepted; the officials can't prove grounding and the quarterback avoids a loss.

**Two-minute drill:** a special series of plays used during the last two minutes of play when a quick touchdown is needed (the hurry-up offense).

**Zone defense:** a pass defense in which each defender is responsible for a specific area of the field.

# AMERICAN FOOTBALL

## SOME INTERESTING NFL RECORDS

| TEAM | RECORD |
| --- | --- |
| Green Bay Packers | Most NFL titles — 11 |
| Pittsburgh Steelers | Most Super Bowl wins — 4 |

| PLAYER | RECORD |
| --- | --- |
| George Blanda | Most points in a career — 2,002 |
| Paul Hornung | Most points in a single season — 176 |
| John Riggins | Most touchdowns in one season — 24 |
| Jim Brown | Most seasons as leading rusher — 8 |
| Walter Payton | Most yards gained rushing in a career — 14,860 |
| Eric Dickerson | Most yards gained in one season rushing — 2,105 |
| Walter Payton | Most yards gained in a single game —275 |
| Jim Brown | Highest average gain per carry rushing in a career —5.2 |
| Jim Brown | Most touchdowns rushing in a career —106 |
| John Riggins | Most touchdowns rushing in a single season — 24 |
| Ernie Nevers | Most touchdowns rushing in a single game — 6 |
| Dan Marino | Most passes completed in a single season — 362 (attempted 564) |
| Richard Todd | Most passes completed in a single game — 42 (attempted 59) |
| Fran Tarkenton | Most yards gained passing in a career — 47,003 |
| Dan Marino | Most yards gained passing in a single season — 5,084 |
| Norm Van Brocklin | Most yards gained passing in a single game — 554 |
| Dan Marino | Most touchdown passes thrown in a single season — 48 |
| Charley Joiner | Most receptions in a career — 716 |
| Art Monk | Most receptions in a single season —106 |
| Tom Fears | Most receptions in a single game — 18 |
| Mark Clayton | Most touchdown pass receptions in a single season — 18 |
| Bob Shaw Kellen Winslow | Most touchdown pass receptions in a single game — 5 |
| Steve O'Neal | Longest punt — 98 yards |
| Warren Moon | Most fumbles in a single game — 7 |

EVERY TEAM HAS A DISTINCT PERSONALITY. THEY'RE A RUNNING TEAM, OR A CONSERVATIVE TEAM, OR A GAMBLING TEAM. ON TOP OF THIS, A TEAM HAS SPECIFIC TENDENCIES. THEY CALL PLAYS MORE OFTEN THAN OTHERS, OR THEY USE CERTAIN PLAYS REGULARLY IN CERTAIN SITUATIONS. COACHES CHANGE THEIR OFFENCE AND DEFENSE TO TAKE ADVANTAGE OF THEIR OPPONENTS' TENDENCIES.

# AMERICAN FOOTBALL

## THE SUPER BOWL RECORDS

| YEAR | WINNER | LOSER | SCORE |
|------|--------|-------|-------|
| 1967 | Green Bay Packers | Kansas City Chiefs | 35-10 |
| 1968 | Green Bay Packers | Oakland Raiders | 33-14 |
| 1969 | New York Jets | Baltimore Colts | 16- 7 |
| 1970 | Kansas City Chiefs | Minnesota Vikings | 23- 7 |
| 1971 | Baltimore Colts | Dallas Cowboys | 16-13 |
| 1972 | Dallas Cowboys | Miami Dolphins | 24- 3 |
| 1973 | Miami Dolphins | Washington Redskins | 14- 7 |
| 1974 | Miami Dolphins | Minnesota Vikings | 24- 7 |
| 1975 | Pittsburgh Steelers | Minnesota Vikings | 16- 6 |
| 1976 | Pittsburgh Steelers | Dallas Cowboys | 21- 7 |
| 1977 | Oakland Raiders | Minnesota Vikings | 32-14 |
| 1978 | Dallas Cowboys | Denver Broncos | 27-10 |
| 1979 | Pittsburgh Steelers | Dallas Cowboys | 35-31 |
| 1980 | Pittsburgh Steelers | Los Angeles Rams | 31-19 |
| 1981 | Oakland Raiders | Philadelphia Eagles | 27-10 |
| 1982 | San Francisco 49ers | Cincinatti Bengals | 26-21 |
| 1983 | Washington Redskins | Miami Dolphins | 27-17 |
| 1984 | Los Angeles Raiders | Washington Redskins | 38- 9 |
| 1985 | San Francisco Raiders | Miami Dolphins | 38-16 |

| PLAYER | RECORD |
|--------|--------|
| Franco Harris | Most points scored in a career — 24 |
| Roger Craig | Most points scored in a single game —18 |
| Franco Harris | Most yards rushing in a career — 354 |
| Marcus Allen | Most yards rushing in a single game —191 |
| Terry Bradshaw | Most yards gained passing in a career — 932 |
| Joe Montana | Most yards gained passing in a single game — 331 |
| Terry Bradshaw | Most touchdown passes thrown in a career — 9 |
| Terry Bradshaw | Most touchdown passes thrown in a single game — 4 |

# AMERICAN FOOTBALL

## OFFICIALS' SIGNALS

**OFFSIDE (ENCROACHMENT):** 5 yards
crossing the line of scrimmage before the ball has been
snapped

**ILLEGAL PROCEDURE:** 5 yards
(covers many different fouls)
—false start: movement by the offense before the snap
—less than 7 players on the line
—taking more than 2 steps after a fair catch
—handing the ball forward
—illegal snap
—improper fair catch signal

**ILLEGAL MOTION:** 5 yards
players moving illegally at the time of the snap

**ILLEGAL SHIFT:** 5 yards
offensive failed to remain stationary for one full second
prior to the snap

**ILLEGAL RETURN:** 5 yards
a substitute entering the game incorrectly or illegally
(after being ejected)

# AMERICAN FOOTBALL

## OFFICIALS' SIGNALS

**DELAY OF GAME:** 5 yards
taking too long to put the ball into play

**PERSONAL FOUL:** 15 yards
a generic term to cover several different fouls: the different infractions are each signalled separately (kneeing, kicking, tripping, piling on)

**CLIPPING:** 15 yards
throwing a block from behind, across the back or legs of an opponent who is not the ball carrier

**ROUGHING THE KICKER:** 15 yards
running into the kicker or kicker's ball holder after the kick

**UNSPORTSMANLIKE CONDUCT:** 15 yards
this call is for both unsportsmanlike conduct and illegal person on the field

**ILLEGAL USE OF HANDS:** 15 yards
a blocker may not use hands to push, pull, or grab an opponent

# AMERICAN FOOTBALL

## OFFICIALS' SIGNALS

◁ **INTENTIONAL GROUNDING:** 5 yards
 passer throws the ball away to avoid taking a loss

**ILLEGAL FORWARD PASS:** 5 yards + loss of down

◁ **PASS OR KICK INTERFERENCE:** 15 yards    penalty is at
 —offensive interference with pass    point of foul
 —defensive pass interference    15 yards
 —fair catch interference

**ILLEGAL RECEIVER DOWNFIELD:** 15 yards

◁ **ILLEGAL KICK:** 5 yards

◁ **ILLEGALLY KICKING, BATTING, OR TOUCHING THE BALL:** 15 yards

**HELPING THE RUNNER:** 10 yards
 pushing or assissting the ball carrier move forward

**CRAWLING:** 5 yards

# AMERICAN FOOTBALL

## GLOSSARY OF TERMS

**BACK:** One of the offensive team in the backfield, that is behind the line. This usually includes the quarterback, fullbacks and halfbacks.
On the defensive team it refers to the safeties, cornerbacks, or linebackers.

**BATTING:** Hitting the ball intentionally. The exception to this as a penalty is on the forward pass or a kick attempt.

LEGAL BLOCK

**BLOCKER:** The player doing the blocking.

BLITZ

**BLITZ:** This is a defensive play in which the linebackers or safeties charge across the line of scrimmage in a surprise attack on the quarterback.

**BLOCK:** This is a term used to describe the action of an offensive player trying to stop the defensive player by legal use of his body (any part of his body above his knees). When using his arms, they must be kept in tight to his body. The offensive player may not use his hands.

**BLOCKED KICK:** A kick that has been stopped or deflected by a defensive player.

**CENTER:** The position in the center of the offensive line. This player initiates the play by snapping the ball.

**CHAIN CREW:** Sometimes called the Chain Gang, these three men are in charge of the yardage chains on the sidelines.

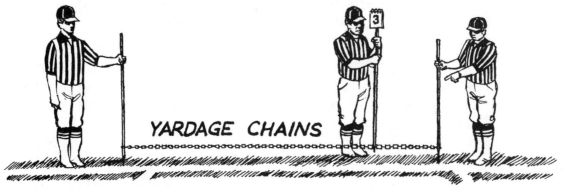

YARDAGE CHAINS

**CLIPPING:** An illegal block in which the blocker runs or dives or throws his body into an opponent's back or the back of his legs (if that player is not the ball carrier). Clipping is legal if done on the line and done within a 3 yard by 4 yard rectangle centered on the middle offensive lineman.

**COMPLETION:** A forward pass that is caught.

**CRAWLING:** An attempt by a player to advance the ball after he has been tackled or the play has been whistled dead.

**CUT:** A quick change of direction by a runner.

**DELAY OF GAME:** Any action that prolongs the game illegally or not being ready to start play within the alotted time.

**DOUBLE FOUL:** When both teams commit infractions in the same down. Often these penalties off-set each other so no yardage is marked off.

**DOWN:** The action of a single play. At the start of play, the offense has four downs in which to advance the ball ten yards. If they are successful, they start at first down again.

**DROP KICK:** The kicker drops the ball to the ground and kicks it as it rebounds.

**ENCROACHMENT:** The defensive term for offside. It is usually a lineman who moves across the neutral zone before the ball is snapped.

**END ZONES:** The area behind the goal posts bounded by the end, side and goal lines.

**EXTRA POINT:** Sometimes referred to as "the point after" because it is attempted after a touchdown has been scored. It is a one play chance for the team that just scored a touchdown to gain an extra point.

**FAIR CATCH:** A receiver of a kicked ball has the opportunity to catch the ball and be protected against being tackled. He indicates he wants a fair catch by raising one arm above his head while the ball is in flight. The receiver may not advance the ball after a fair catch.

**FIELD GOAL:** A three-point score gained by place-kicking or drop-kicking the ball over the opponent's crossbar and between the uprights from behind the line of scrimmage.

**FORWARD PASS:** A pass thrown from in or behind the neutral zone, downfield toward the opponent's goal line. Only the offense may throw a forward pass.

**FOUL:** An infraction of a rule.

**FUMBLE:** A ball dropped by a player and is still in play. That is a fumbled ball can be picked up and run with.

**GOAL LINE:** This line marks the beginning of the end zone and the end of the playing field. There is one goal line at each end of the field. The plane of the goal line must be crossed for a score to take place.

**HALFTIME:** A 15 minute break in play between the halves. The game is divided into four 15 minute quarters. There are two quarters in each half.

# AMERICAN FOOTBALL

**HANDOFF:** The handing of the ball from one offensive player to another. Handoffs are used in offensive play to confuse, surprise or otherwise get past the defense.

**INTENTIONAL GROUNDING:** A rule infraction caused when a passer deliberately throws the ball away in a fake forward pass to avoid being tackled for a loss.

*HANDOFF*

**HUDDLE:** This is the team "meeting" prior to a play where the signals and the play are given. The huddle is usually a loose circle of players.

**ILLEGAL PROCEDURE:** A penalty called against the offense for movement on the line after the ball has been set and before it has been snapped. While the quarterback is calling out the signals, the offensive linemen must remain still.

**IN-BOUND LINES:** Two sets of lines running on both sides of the field, 70 feet, 9 inches from the side lines.

**INCOMPLETION:** An incomplete forward pass.

**INELIGIBLE RECEIVER:** Any offensive player not legally able to catch a forward pass (usually an inside tackle, a guard, or the center).

**INTERCEPTION:** A pass caught by an opponent. Their player may run with the ball

**KICK-OFF:** The kick used to start play at the start of the game, at the beginning of the second half, and after each score.

**LATERAL:** Also called a backward pass, this is a pass that goes back from or parallel to the line of scrimmage. Any player may throw a lateral pass at any time to any teammate.

**LINE OF SCRIMMAGE:** An imaginary line that runs from side line to side line, parallel to the goal lines, and passing through the end of the ball. There are two lines of scrimmage, one for each team. The space between them is the neutral zone.

**LOOSE BALL:** A live ball, that is a ball in play, but not in any player's possession.

**MAN IN MOTION:** One offensive back can move as or before the ball is snapped. He must, though, move back from or parallel to his line of scrimmage. Before he starts, the back must be at least one yard behind the line of scrimmage.

**MULTIPLE FOULS:** Two or more fouls committed by the same team in the same down. The opposing team has the choice of which penalty shall be assessed.

**NEUTRAL ZONE:** The area between the two lines of scrimmage and is the width of the football.

**OFFENSE:** The team in possession of the ball.

**OFFENSIVE HOLDING:** An offensive player illegally using his hands while blocking a defensive player.

**OFFSIDE:** A penalty caused by a player crossing the line of scrimmage before the ball is snapped.

**ONSIDE KICK:** A play by the kicking team to try and regain control of the ball after the kick. It's a short kick, just over ten yards if possible. In actual fact, all kicks are "onside", but this term refers to this specific type of kick.

**OUT-OF-BOUNDS:** The area outside the sidelines and endlines. The lines themselves are out-of-bounds also, therefore if a player or the ball touches or crosses these lines it is out-of-bounds.

**PASS INTERFERENCE:** Any act that interferes with a player's chance to catch a pass or to intercept a pass.

**PENALTY MARKER:** A yellow flag thrown down by an official to indicate a rule infraction has occurred.

**PERSONAL FOUL:** Hitting, punching, kneeing, piling on, clipping, unnecessary roughness, or running into the passer or the kicker.

KNEEING

ELBOWING

SPEARING

KICKING

**PILING ON:** Jumping or falling on a downed player after the play has been whistled dead.

**PLACE KICK:** A kick where the ball is held in place by a teammate or a kicking tee.

**POCKET:** A shield set up by the five interior linemen on the offensive team around the quarterback to protect him while he sets up to throw a forward pass.

**POSSESSION:** The officials must determine when a player has possession of the ball. It is defined as having control of the ball long enough to perform any act common to the game.

**PUNT:** A kick made by dropping the ball and kicking it before it hits the ground.

**PUNT RETURN:** The runback made by the team after catching a punt.

**QUARTER:** A 15 minute section of the game. There are four quarters in a game.

**RECOVER:** Gain possession of the ball after a fumble.

**RETURN:** The runback of a kick or an intercepted pass.

**RUNNING PLAY:** A play from the line of scrimmage where no pass is involved.

**SACK:** To dump the quarterback for a loss while he is attempting a forward pass. The defensive players exalt in sacking the quarterback.

**SAFETY:** A two point score made by the team not in possession of the ball. It happens when the offensive team causes the ball to end up behind their own goal line themselves.

**SCRIMMAGE:** The action of a play beginning at the snap and ending when the ball is whistled dead.

**SHIFT:** This is the movement of two or more offensive players changing positions at the same time before the ball is snapped.

**SNAP:** The passing of the ball by the center to a back usually the quarterback.

*THE SNAP*

# AMERICAN FOOTBALL

**SPEARING:** Lunging at a player with your helmet in an attempt to injure him.

**TACKLE:** A defensive player using his hands, arms, or body to stop the ball carrier.

**TIME-OUT:** A stoppage in play during which the official game clock is stopped.

**TOUCHBACK:** When the offensive team stops the play in the defensive team's end zone, the ball is brought out to the 20 yard line to start play. This can happen after a kick-off or a punt.

**TOUCHDOWN:** A six-point score when the ball carrier reaches the end zone of the opposing team. This can happen by running into the end zone, catching a pass in the end zone or recovering a fumble in the end zone.

**TRY-FOR-POINT:** A team that has just scored a touchdown gets one play to put the ball into the opponent's end zone again for extra points. If they place kick the ball between the uprights and above the crossbar, they score one extra point. If they run or pass the ball into the end zone, they score two extra points.

**TURNOVER:** Losing the ball to the opponents by fumbling or giving up an interception.

**TWO-MINUTE WARNING:** This is a time-out called by the officials while they tell each head coach that only two minutes remain in the half.

**YARDAGE:** The number of yards gained or lost by either team or any player.

TOUCHDOWN

PRINTED IN CANA